ABOUT THE EDITORS

Marshall Sashkin is a senior associate in the Office of Educational Research and Improvement, the U.S. Department of Education's research applications arm, where he helps develop and guide applied research to improve schools. He earned his doctorate in organizational psychology from the University of Michigan and has taught at various institutions. From 1979 to 1984 he was a professor of industrial and organizational psychology at the University of Maryland. He is currently an adjunct professor of psychology and administrative sciences at George Washington University.

Sashkin has conducted research and published in the areas of leadership, participation, and organizational change. He is author or co-author of more than ten books and monographs, and of fifty research reports. His work has appeared in the *Psychological Review,* the *Journal of Applied Psychology*, the *Academy of Management Review,* and other research publications. For seven years he served as editor of the research and practice journal *Group & Organization Studies* and is now an assistant editor of the ASTD-sponsored research journal *Human Resource Development Quarterly.*

Herbert J. Walberg is Research Professor of Education at the University of Illinois at Chicago. A member of the presidentially created New American Schools Research and Development Corporation, he has served as an advisor on educational research and improvement to public and private agencies in the United States and a dozen other countries.

He has written or edited numerous books and has contributed many articles to educational, psychological, and practitioner journals on such topics as giftedness and talent development, educational productivity, international comparisons, instruction, and parent education. He has also written frequently for widely circulated journals such as *Daedalus, Educational Leadership, Kappan,* and *Nature,* and for many newspapers.

D1442382

EDUCATIONAL LEADERSHIP AND SCHOOL CULTURE

The Series on Contemporary Educational Issues
Kenneth J. Rehage, Series Editor

The 1993 Titles

Motivating Students to Learn: Overcoming Barriers to High Achievement,
edited by Tommy M. Tomlinson
Educational Leadership and School Culture, edited by Marshall
Sashkin and Herbert J. Walberg

The Ninety-second Yearbook of the National Society for the Study
of Education, published in 1993, contains two volumes:

Gender and Education, edited by Sari Knopp Biklen and Diane Pollard
Bilingual Education: Politics, Practice, and Research, edited by
M. Beatriz Arias and Ursula Casanova

All members of the Society receive its two-volume Yearbook.
Members who take the Comprehensive Membership also receive
the two current volumes in the Series on Contemporary
Educational Issues.

Membership in the Society is open to any who desire to receive its
publications. Inquiries regarding membership, including current
dues, may be addressed to the Secretary-Treasurer, NSSE, 5835
Kimbark Ave., Chicago, IL 60637.

EDUCATIONAL LEADERSHIP AND SCHOOL CULTURE

EDITED BY

MARSHALL SASHKIN

Office of Educational Research and Improvement
U.S. Department of Education

AND

HERBERT J. WALBERG

University of Illinois at Chicago

McCutchan Publishing Corporation
2940 San Pablo Ave., P.O. Box 774, Berkeley, CA 94701

ISBN 0–8211–1861–7
Library of Congress Catalog Card Number 92–85142

Printed in the United States of America

CONTENTS

CONTRIBUTORS

Carole Ames is Professor of Education and Chair of the Department of Educational Psychology at the University of Illinois, Urbana-Champaign.

Russell Ames was formerly Professor of Educational Leadership and Research Director and Principal of University High School at the University of Illinois, Urbana-Champaign. He is currently a clinical counseling psychologist in private practice.

Rachel Buck is a doctoral student at the University of Michigan.

Terrence E. Deal is Professor of Education, Peabody College of Vanderbilt University, and Co-director of the National Center for Educational Leadership.

Judith L. Endeman is Superintendent of Schools of the Ramona Unified School District, Ramona, California.

William A. Firestone is a Professor in the Graduate School of Education at Rutgers University and Director of the Center for Educational Policy Analysis in New Jersey.

Samuel E. Krug is President of MetriTech, Inc., in Champaign, Illinois.

Martin L. Maehr is Professor of Education and Psychology and Director of the Combined Program in Education and Psychology in the Horace H. Rackham School of Graduate Studies at the University of Michigan.

Kent D. Peterson is Professor of Education at the University of Wisconsin, Madison.

Marshall Sashkin is Senior Associate in the Office of Educational Research and Improvement, U. S. Department of Education, Washington, D.C.

Molly G. Sashkin is a career counselor and organizational consultant in private practice in Seabrook, Maryland.

Thomas J. Sergiovanni is Radford Professor of Education and Administration at Trinity University, San Antonio, Texas.

Herbert J. Walberg is Research Professor of Education at the University of Illinois at Chicago.

Bruce L. Wilson is Program Director, Research for Better Schools, Philadelphia, Pennsylvania.

PREFACE

Leadership is hardly a new topic to school administrators. For more than a generation we have heard calls for stronger and more effective leadership, both in the school building and at the school district level. Indeed, Bossert (1985), in his review of what makes for effective secondary schools, specifically identifies strong leadership as one of a handful of crucial causal factors. In this judgment Bossert echoes many of those who have contributed to what has come to be called the "effective schools" approach.

It is more recently that educators' focus has expanded to include the concept of "culture" (Deal and Kennedy, 1982). Yet "school culture" is rapidly becoming as widespread a term as school leadership. Many of the authors represented in this volume have been at the forefront of the study of school culture.

What is only now beginning to be recognized is the fact that leadership and culture are intimately linked, are cause and effect, in deep and important ways. Edgar H. Schein, an organizational psychologist at the Massachusetts Institute of Technology's Sloan School of Management, has pioneered in the study of organizational culture and leadership. He has said that it may well be that the *only* important thing that leaders do is construct culture (Schein, 1985).

If we are to work toward improving schools, one thing is clear: we need a much better understanding of school culture, educational leadership, and the ways they are interrelated. That is the premise and the structure of this book.

The book is divided into three sections. Section 1 explores the nature of organizational culture, particularly school cultures, since the central activities of education—teaching and learning—occur within schools and classrooms. Section 2 analyzes leadership, with a focus on what is called "visionary" or "transformational" leadership. It is this newly identified form of leadership, not the traditional concept of leadership as supervision, that is needed by those who would shape school cultures so as to support educational excellence. Section 3 analyzes the relation between leadership and culture. In this concluding integrative section the authors attempt to show what forms, styles, and practices of leadership have the greatest promise for constructing school cultures that promote excellence.

To underscore the contribution of each chapter to its section and to the book as a whole, we provide here an overview of the highlights of each chapter.

THE NATURE OF EDUCATIONAL CULTURE

In addressing the question "What is school culture?" Terrence Deal, in Chapter 1, alludes to Willard Waller's writings of the early 1930s. School culture was then and is now distinctive, powerful, pervasive, and enduring. As in corporate and other cultures, educational culture implies shared values, heroes, rituals, ceremonies, stories, and networks. Because cultures can be so compelling, they may resist internally or externally perceived needs for change. Yet to respond to educators' needs for professional autonomy and society's demands for improvements, institutions must attempt to change their cultures and practices. Deal describes how continuity and change may be accomplished by such practices as articulating shared values, re-creating school histories, and reinvigorating rituals and ceremonies.

In Chapter 4, "Bureaucratic and Cultural Linkages: Implications for the Principal," William Firestone and Bruce Wilson describe two different but important ways that principals influence instruction. Bureaucratic linkages create or limit opportunities for teacher discretion; principals' formal decisions may be used to modify them. Cultural linkages affect the ways teachers think about their work; principals' symbolic activities may be used to modify them. Principals' control of a few dramatic actions as well as coordination of smaller cumulative acts can serve to influence instruction constructively. Extramural linkages, both bureaucratic and cultural, also bear upon instruction as illustrated in state testing policies and reports of commissions advocating reform.

In Chapter 3, "Transforming School Culture," Martin Maehr and Rachel Buck argue that the wide variety of recent reforms in educational governance have not yielded constructive changes. Such reforms, they argue, are superficial; they have not touched the deep cultural values that are best revealed by the educators' motivation and behavior. The authors point out that educators need to express their goals more clearly, modify curriculum and instructional practices, give students greater responsibility, alter the reward system, avoid ability grouping and invidious competition, and modify the schedule of the school day. Maehr and Buck discuss strategies for implementing such far-reaching changes.

THE NATURE OF LEADERSHIP

Thomas Sergiovanni, in "New Sources of Leadership Authority" (Chapter 4), attributes the failure of leadership to the sacrifice of spiritual values for psychological gains, and to the neglect of moral and professional ideals in attaining technical authority. He argues that experience, intuition, and emotions should play a large role in leadership, and that leaders should avoid relying solely on science and deductive logic. Sergiovanni questions the purely technical approaches to leadership and shows how professional authority and experience can be more effectively exercised.

In Chapter 5, "The Visionary Principal: School Leadership for the Next Century," Marshall Sashkin argues that cultural leadership can be exerted in schools through changes in atmosphere, expectations, goals, communications, and parent and community connections. He notes, however, that systematic change also requires visionary leaders who can help educational professionals adapt to their environments, integrate internal activities into a cohesive whole, and set forth and concentrate on achievable goals. Sashkin illustrates how these ideals can be accomplished through the visions school leaders develop and the practices in which they engage.

THE RELATION OF CULTURE AND LEADERSHIP

Terrence Deal and Kent Peterson in Chapter 6, "Strategies for Building School Cultures: Principals as Symbolic Leaders," concentrate on what William Firestone and Bruce Wilson in Chapter 2 called the building of cultural linkages. In the first chapter of this book, Deal speaks in rather broad and general terms about school culture—while he states clearly that building culture is a crucial task of leaders, he does not provide much in the way of specific guidelines for action to do so. In Chapter 6, Deal and Peterson give just such a set of guidelines for leaders who would go about the important and difficult task of culture building. Their advice is based on an intensive analysis of case studies of leaders who engaged successfully in culture-building activities.

In Chapter 7, "Principals and Their School Cultures: Under-standings from Quantitative and Qualitative Research," Marshall Sashkin and Molly Sashkin describe how educational leadership and culture may be assessed, using several questionnaire measures. Their work in a dozen schools shows significant connections between vision-ary leadership and school culture. Their case studies show how such connections can be developed through such strategies as value-based staffing, constructive use of conflict, and modeling values in action. Samuel Krug, in Chapter 10, makes clear his view that quantitative measurement is essential for understanding leadership and culture building, and Sashkin and Sashkin agree. But they also agree with Deal and Peterson that by analyzing and understanding qualitative data one can gain much in the way of *practical* understanding. In their chapter Sashkin and Sashkin not only explore the quantitative assess-ment of leadership and culture, they also attempt to integrate this quantitative understanding with a qualitative approach that is fo-cused on applications.

In Chapter 8, "Creating a Mastery-Oriented Schoolwide Culture: A Team Leadership Perspective," Russell Ames and Carole Ames describe site-based management (SBM) as a second and promising wave of educational reform. They outline SBM's theoretical underpinnings in communication research that requires production, maintenance, and innovation. From the psychological viewpoint, however, individual motivation is critical in implementing SBM programs. Ames and Ames show how motivation, culture, and instructional practices can be measured and improved by educational leaders.

In Chapter 9, "Visionary Superintendents and Their Districts," Judith Endeman extends the leadership-culture link to the school district level. She compares two similar groups of school districts, one group characterized by superintendents assessed as visionary leaders and the other with superintendents who are not so visionary. Ende-man finds strong evidence of major differences in district culture between districts in the two groups, suggesting that the superinten-dent's leadership does make a difference. She also finds some hints of differences in students' performance on measures of outcomes.

In the final chapter, "Leadership and Culture: A Quantitative Perspective on School Leadership and Instructional Climate," Samuel Krug describes an extensive program of research and educational intervention aimed at developing valid measures of leadership and culture. His extensive review of the literature, including his own current research, leads him to a number of important insights on the relative contributions of quantitative and qualitative approaches to research on school culture.

In our brief concluding note we offer a synthesis of several of the major perspectives. We hope that these introductory highlights whet the reader's appetite for the chapters and that our framework for understanding them proves useful.

Marshall Sashkin
Herbert J. Walberg

REFERENCES

Bossert, Steven T. "Effective Elementary Schools." In *Reaching for Excellence: An Effective Schools Sourcebook*, edited by Regina M. J. Kyle. Washington, DC: U. S. Government Printing Office, 1985.

Deal, Terrence, and Kennedy, Allan.   *Corporate Cultures: The Rites and Rituals of Corporate Life.* Reading, Mass.: Addison-Wesley, 1982.

Schein, Edgar H. *Organizational Culture and Leadership*. San Francisco: Jossey-Bass, 1985.

Section I

The Nature of School Culture

Chapter 1

THE CULTURE OF SCHOOLS

Terrence E. Deal

Albert Shanker, head of the American Federation of Teachers, succinctly captured the power of culture in schools and classrooms:

> Ten thousand new teachers each year enter the New York City school system as a result of retirement, death, job turnover, and attrition. These new teachers come from all over the country. They represent all religions, races, political persuasions, and educational institutions. But the amazing thing is that after three weeks in the classroom you can't tell them apart from the teachers they replaced.

The classroom embodies a powerful script. The stage, props, actors, and costumes can vary slightly from level to level, from time to time, or from place to place. But the key roles and the central drama are almost the same—even in other cultures. A classroom is a classroom is a classroom. Schools also show a remarkable consistency across time and national boundaries (Meyer and Rowan, 1983). A recent visit to a high school convinced me that my twenty-year absence from a secondary classroom made little difference. An afternoon in a Japanese high school several years ago also seemed remarkably familiar. If I had spoken Japanese, I could easily have taken the place of the teacher whose class I observed. The campuses of both schools were similar and bore an uncanny resemblance to those I remember as a student and teacher.

How can we account for the dependability and durability of

Reprinted with the permission of the Association for Supervision and Curriculum Development. From *Leadership: Examining the Elusive*, 1987 ASCD Yearbook, edited by Linda Shieve and Marion Schoenheit. Alexandria, Va.: Association for Supervision and Curriculum Development, 1987. (Pp. 3–15.) Copyright 1987 by ASCD.

educational practices? Despite the number of current theories, no one
seems able to explain why the patterns exist or what we can do to
make them different. If the recent spate of commission reports is
accurate, American education is failing dismally and in fact is in a
state of crisis. Has the time come to break the cosmic classroom? Or
do we need to refine or recharge existing practices? In either case, we
need first to understand why the patterns are so stable and immune to
change.

Waller (1932) offered a powerful insight several decades ago:

Schools have a culture that is definitely their own. There are, in the school, complex
rituals of personal relationships, a set of folkways, mores, and irrational sanctions, a
moral code based upon them. There are games, which are sublimated wars, teams,
and an elaborate set of ceremonies concerning them. There are traditions, and
traditionalists waging their world-old battle against innovators. There are laws and
there is a problem of enforcing them, there is *Sittlichkeit*. [P. 103]

Sarason [1971] and Swidler (1979) recently echoed Waller's insights. Swidler noted:

Watching teachers and students in free schools, I become convinced that culture in
the sense of symbols, ideologies, and a legitimate language for discussing individual
and group obligations provides the crucial substrate on which new organizational
forms can be erected. . . . Organizational innovations and cultural change are constantly intertwined, since it is culture that creates the new images of human nature
and new symbols with which people can move one another. [P. viii]

Two observations from different times, each developed by independent researchers examining very different samples: Waller (1932)
looked mainly at traditional schools; Swidler (1979), decades later,
studied alternative schools. Their common imagery suggests what the
arduous struggle over changing schools and classrooms is really all
about. Images of schools and beliefs and assumptions about schooling
are encoded early in our experience. The images and beliefs arise from
and are tied to a human culture stable over time, largely hidden from
conscious view.

In this sense, starting a school from scratch is impossible. Even
innovators carry imprints in their heads. Entering any school evokes a
predictable script and reciprocal roles. These imprints serve as the
basis for educational rituals, the foundation of educational practice.

Parents and communities also carry the imprints. The school is a symbol. It needs the right trappings: a flag, a principal, teachers, students, desks, and a curriculum. Those outside assume that those inside are following the script—unless they have reason to believe otherwise (Meyer and Rowan, 1983). This shared culture of schools and classrooms gives meaning to the process of education. The same stable implicit pattern frustrates efforts to improve, reform, or change educational forms and practices at all levels.

WHAT IS CULTURE?

We believe that goals, technical logic, and evaluation govern our modern world. Often, however, they do not. Beneath the façade lurks another world, a primordial place of myths, fairy tales, ceremonies, heroes, and demons—the primitive world that modern ways reputedly left behind. Yet it remains a powerful force behind the scenes in modern organizations. We call them corporations; primitive people called them tribes.

In education, several researchers have tried to conceptualize the elusive symbolic side of schools and classrooms: ethos (Rutter et al., 1979), saga (Clark, 1975), and climate (McDill and Rigsby, 1973; Halpin and Croft, 1962). The concept of culture has also received some attention. Waller (1932), for example, described the school culture:

Teachers have always known that it was not necessary for the students of strange customs to cross the seas to find material. Folklore and myth, tradition, taboo, magic rites, ceremonials of all sorts, collective representations, participation mystique all abound in the front yard of every school, and occasionally they creep upstairs and are incorporated into the more formal portions of school life. [P. 103]

Sarason (1971) depicted a similar phenomenon using a different language. He wrote of behavioral regularities and a restricted universe of alternatives. People behave the same in schools and see no real options.

The problem [of change inheres] in the fact that history and tradition have given rise to roles and relationships, to interlocking ideas, practices, values, and expectations that are the "givens" not requiring thought or deliberation. These "givens" (like other categories of thought) are far less the products of characteristics of individuals than they are a reflection of what we call the culture and its traditions. . . . One of the most difficult obstacles to recognizing that the major problems in our schools inhere far less in the characteristics of individuals than it does in [the school's] cultural and system characteristics is that one cannot *see* culture or system the way one sees individuals. Culture and system are not concrete, tangible, visible things the way individuals are. [Pp. 227–228]

The recent application of culture to modern corporations has spawned still another generation of definitions. Deal and Kennedy (1982) relied on *Webster's*:

[Culture is] the integrated pattern of human behavior that includes thought, speech, action, artifacts, and depends on man's capacity for learning and transmitting knowledge to succeeding generations.

Formal definitions, though verifiable and rigorous, often fail to capture the robustness of a concept as experienced by those who know it firsthand. Culture is an all-encompassing tapestry of meaning. Culture is "the way we do things around here." The ways are trans-mitted from generation to generation. Culture is learned (Deal and Kennedy, 1982). McPherson (1972) illustrated the process of cultural transmission in her intensive observation of rural schools:

Among teachers: "For the old guard teachers, tradition was the key symbol. What I learned in training school or what has always been done. The present is always judged by how it 'used to be done.' Since the past was always far rosier than the present."

Between teacher and students: "To the frequent pupil objection, 'But that's not the way Mrs. Smith did it', she would respond, 'But you are in fifth grade now. We do it this way'." [P. 56]

Tangible cultural forms embody or represent the ways of a people, or a classroom, or a school:

- *Shared values*—shorthand slogans that summarize deep-seated core values: "IBM Means Service": "The H-P Way"; "Progress Is Our Most Important Product"; "*Veritas.*"
- *Heroes*—the pantheon of individuals who embody or represent core values: Lee Iaccoca, Mary Kay Ashe, John DeLorean, or Angus McDonald, whose efforts to restore service in the blizzard of 1881 are legendary in the Bell System.

- *Rituals*—repetitive behavioral repertoire in which values are experienced directly through implicit signals: the surgical scrub, planning, teaching, the police roll call in *Hill Street Blues*.
- *Ceremonies*—episodic occasions in which the values and heroes are put on display, annointed, and celebrated: the seminars of Mary Kay cosmetics, Hospital Corporation of America's annual meeting, graduation day in schools and universities across the United States.
- *Stories*—concrete examples of values and heroes who triumph by following the culturally prescribed ways: the MacDonald's franchisee who invented the Egg McMuffin and the McD. L. T.; James Burke, chief executive officer of Johnson & Johnson, and how he handled the Tylenol crisis; the principal of the "Magic Mayo" school in Tulsa, Oklahoma, and how she has created an exciting learning environment.
- *Cultural network*—a collection of informal priest/esses, gossips, spies, and storytellers whose primary role is to reinforce and to protect the existing ways: no examples are needed; everyone knows who they are.

Culture as a construct helps explain why classrooms and schools exhibit common and stable patterns across variable conditions. Internally, culture gives meaning to instructional activity and provides a symbolic bridge between action and results. It fuses individual identity with collective destiny. Externally, culture provides the symbolic façade that evokes faith and confidence among outsiders with a stake in education (Meyer and Rowan, 1983).

THE MORE THINGS CHANGE, THE MORE THEY STAY THE SAME

Sarason (1971) echoed a phrase that summarizes our experience in trying to change education: The harder we try, the less schools and classrooms seem to change. Several explanations have been offered, each with an accompanying remedy (Bolman and Deal, 1984). The most popular explanation focuses on the problem of individual resistance (Baldridge and Deal, 1983): Schools are tough to change because professionals lack the required skills and are negatively disposed toward change. To cope with the problem in the past, we have either relied heavily on training or tried to "people proof" innovations.

A second explanation emphasizes the formal structure of schools and classrooms (Corwin, 1972; Baldridge and Deal, 1983): Changes fail because roles are improperly defined or because adequate levels of interdependence and coordination do not exist. This logic has spawned efforts to redefine roles, to create teams, or to build the problem-solving capacity of schools.

A third explanation evokes the law of the jungle (Baldridge, 1975): Desired changes fall short because they threaten the balance of power, create opposing coalitions, and trigger conflict. Political remedies have focused on co-opting the opposition, building coalitions to support innovations, or bargaining among warring camps to reach an agreeable compromise or truce.

While each of these perspectives is useful, none adequately pinpoints the key problem of change. Remedies derived from these theories have not altered the modal experience of changing. We still do not fully understand the process of introducing new ways into existing social systems.

CULTURE AND CHANGE: A BASIC CONTRADICTION

Looking at the problem of change through a cultural lens, we see an entirely different picture. Culture is a social invention created to give meaning to human endeavor. It provides stability, certainty, and predictability. People fear ambiguity and want assurance that they are in control of their surroundings. Culture imbues life with meaning and through symbols creates a sense of efficacy and control. Change creates existential havoc because it introduces disequilibrium, uncertainty, and makes day-to-day life chaotic and unpredictable. People understandably feel threatened and out of control when their existential pillars become shaky or are taken away.

On an even more basic level, change involves existential loss (Marris, 1974). People become emotionally attached to symbols and rituals, much as they do to lovers, spouses, children, and pets (Deal, 1985b). When attachments to people or objects are broken through death or departure, people experience a deep sense of loss and grief. Change creates a similar reaction. A new principal replaces a cherished hero. Mr. Smith, a beloved maverick, leaves teaching for a high-paying position in business. Miss Dove, whose demands and discipline are legendary, takes early retirement because she cannot cope with innovative methods. The computer alters the relationship between teacher and student. Small discussion groups replace classroom lecture and recitation. A graduation ceremony is changed to conform to modern standards. A well-known gossip is transferred to another school, or the popular storyteller suddenly dies.

People develop attachments to values, heroes, rituals, ceremonies, stories, gossips, storytellers, priests, and other cultural players. When change alters or breaks the attachment, meaning is questioned. Often, the change deeply affects those inside the culture as well as those outside. Think of the trauma a school closing or the introduction of the "new math" causes parents. The existential explanation identifies the basic problems of change in educational organizations as cultural transitions.

As a simple illustration, consider the mutual bond that forms between teacher and students:

As the teacher molded her class and was molded by it, she began to identify herself with it. . . . The original separation of interests, the class as they, as the outgrouping, began to fade away and the formerly imperial rights and obligations become imbued with affect. The teacher, spending six hours a day with her class, began to see the world through its eyes, its interests as her interests, even though she continued to be separated from the pupils because of her authority and the requirement that she must teach, judge, and control them. [McPherson, 1972, pp. 112–113]

At the end of each school year, the attachment is broken. Both teacher and students experience a loss. Deep-down, the mourning occurs over the summer. Next year's teacher or class will require a transition period before the loss can be repaired. For some, it never is.

Unresolved change and grief either mire people in the past or trap them in the meaningless present. The unhealed wounds following a change can weaken individuals, classrooms, or schools. To heal the wounds and repair ruptured meaning, cultures need to convene transition rituals, to bury and mourn what has been lost, and then to celebrate the new forms that begin to emerge.

In one elementary school in Massachusetts, for example, students held a ceremony and named the corridors after teachers terminated in the wake of cutbacks caused by a taxpayers' revolt. In another Massachusetts school, the faculty convened to pull itself together in the aftermath of the same circumstances. Before the teachers began to discuss the next steps, the principal stepped to the blackboard and asked them to list what the school had lost. The teachers began to list people, programs, and other tangible things that reduced funds had taken away. As the list grew, the tears came. After an emotional hour and a half, the mood of the group began to change. People focused on their emerging strengths—school spirit, top people, adequate facilities. In the transition event, they let go and were ready to move ahead.

Change is difficult because it alters cultural forms that give meaning to schools and classrooms. For change to work, transition rituals are required to transform meaning, to graft new starts onto old roots.

CULTURAL AND EDUCATIONAL PRODUCTIVITY

Corporations across the United States are reexamining and focusing on the culture of the workplace. Culture has become a preoccupation of management because cultural patterns have been conceptually and empirically linked with performance, morale, turnover, image, and other important business concerns (Peters and Waterman, 1982; Deal and Kennedy, 1982). When someone at IBM is asked what she does for a living, most likely she would respond confidently, "I work for IBM." She responds that way because her identity is fused with the culture of the company. It is the same in other existentially sound businesses.

Compare the culture of IBM with the culture of schools, an IBMer with a classroom teacher. When teachers are asked what they do for a living, many timidly respond, "I'm just a teacher." Their response may reflect a long-term unraveling of the fabric that gives meaning to the process of learning. Where cultures are cohesive, people contribute their efforts toward a common destiny, rallying around shared values that give meaning to work—and to their lives. When cultures are fragmented, people "do their jobs," worry about salaries, and spend their time struggling for power.

In the field of education, two decades of criticism, desegregation, innovation, and frustration have eroded faith and confidence in schools. In the 1960s, researchers claimed that schools did not make a difference (Coleman, 1966). The 1960s and 1970s witnessed a barrage of innovations designed to transform education in countless and contradictory ways: new math, alternative schools, management by objectives (MBO). The accountability movement of the 1970s asked educators to provide measurable evidence of learning and mandated rigorous approaches for evaluating people and results. During these decades, schools were asked to solve the problems of the society, but to make their solutions inexpensive. Schools have been soundly criticized for not accomplishing feats that lie outside the ability of the society to perform. These have been turbulent times for educators, and there is no reason to believe that the turbulence will subside in the near future. Witness the new round of criticism and reform.

The real loser in all this turmoil has been the culture of schools. Outsiders lost faith; many professionals have lost confidence in themselves and their practices. What are the shared values of education that various groups can unite behind? If we ask principals, teachers, students, custodians, or parents what a particular school stands for, can they reply, and do their replies create a chorus or a cacophony of individual voices? Who are educational visionaries? Who are the heroes of our schools, and what values do they represent? Are they anointed and celebrated, or are they basically ignored? Who was the last principal or teacher fired for championing a desirable virtue? How meaningful and alive are faculty meetings, parent get-togethers, classrooms, and other cultural rituals? Waller (1932) described the opening exercises of a high school long ago:

When I was in C____High School, we always began the day with "opening exercises." This was the invariable custom, and the daily grind began in every schoolroom with a few minutes, from a quarter to a half-hour, devoted to singing and pleasant speech-making.

Directly, the last bell had sounded, the principal called us to order by clapping his hands together. There was a last-minute scurrying to seats, a hasty completion of whispered conversations. The principal stood on the platform in the front of the room and watched us. His assistant, Miss W., whom we all knew to be the kindliest of souls, but whom we nevertheless feared as if she were the devil herself, stood up behind her desk and regarded us coldly.

When the room was quiet, the principal turned to the music teacher, Miss M., and said, "All right. Go ahead, Miss M."

Miss M. advanced enthusiastically and announced, "We will begin with number 36 in the paper books. That's an old favorite. Now please, let's all sing." [P. 122]

How do schools begin the day now? How memorable and dramatic are opening-day ceremonies, back-to-school nights, graduation, and other cultural ceremonies? What stories do professionals tell each other? What stories circulate in the local community? Many times, the stories about schools are negative, though they should communicate and dramatize the sacred values of education. Consider the following story:

In a large university, a professor was given tenure and promoted to full professor based in large part on an extensive record of publication. It was learned later that many of his publications had been fabricated. The president of the university learned of the fraud and summoned the professor before a schoolwide committee. He announced his decision about the professor's promotion. "You may keep your tenure and your work, but for two years you can have no contact with students. This is the most severe penalty a teacher can receive."

Stories like this one exist in every school and classroom. Why aren't they told? Who are education's storytellers? Where are the educational priests who worry about sacred values and ceremonial occasions?

In business, the connection between culture and performance is commonly accepted. In schools, where the product is complex and intangible, a strong cohesive culture is even more important than in business. The Rutter and others (1979) study of the relationship between school characteristics and productivity identified ethos as a powerful factor in educational performance. In the effective schools research, Deal (1985a) clearly interpreted many of the characteristics related to performance in cultural terms.

Looking beyond the research into the patterns of a typical school, we can see how culture affects performance. Why should students attend class, come on time, or stay in school if they do not identify with its values? How can we expect students to commit themselves to schoolwork when the student subculture rewards popularity, deviance, or athletic prowess? How can a teacher whose loyalties are tied to a union and whose identity is fused mainly with family or another job be expected to put his heart into the classroom? How can he survive the loneliness of teaching without some support from shared values and schoolwide events? How can a new teacher learn the profession without heroes as role models or stories as exemplars? How can a principal shape a culture when her time is tied to complex procedures for observing the classroom? Why should principals spend time walking around or working on values when they are rewarded for the punctuality and appearance of paperwork? Why should parents and community support schools when their recollections of schools are more poignant than their contemporary observations?

One haunting experience in a school summarized the problem for me. I was in a district as an evaluator. My charge was to assess how well new evaluation procedures were working in individual schools. Sitting in one of those small chairs in a second-grade classroom, I was interviewing a teacher. I was asking rational questions; she was giving sensible answers. Suddenly, memories of my second-grade teacher and classroom flooded my mind. The same sounds, smells, and artifacts. I looked over toward the blackboard, and there it was—the wire chalk holder used to make the music staff. I pulled it across the board to make the five lines. I turned to the teacher and asked her how to make a treble cleff. She quickly jumped to her feet, and I took my chair. It was exactly like my second-grade experience.

I said, "That was magic. You must be proud to be a teacher." Her entire posture and expression changed. She talked eloquently about her work and profession for twenty minutes—values, stories, rituals, ceremonies. She was experiencing the culture. I asked her why she hadn't talked to me like that before. "You are from Harvard, and I didn't think you would care about such things," she said. "Why should you? No one here does." I asked her how the evaluation process was linked to the core values of teaching she had just expressed. She said there was no relationship between the criteria and the important aspects of teaching: "I go along to keep them happy."

From this event, I got a sense of what has happened to the productivity of schools. Students find meaning in their subcultures. Teachers find meaning in unions and friends. Principals derive meaning from modern management ideologies and promotions. Superintendents dream of finding meaning in a larger district. Parents anchor their meaning in family and work, and on it goes across different groups—individual islands with no common glue to tie them together. The absence of cohesion in many schools is no one's fault. The erosion is the result of two decades of turmoil and foment that has eclipsed the real reasons schools and classrooms exist. The current interest in schools provides an exciting opportunity to rebuild the culture of schools and to reinforce the age-old values and practices that give meaning to the process of education. It is a matter of fusing old with new and celebrating the transformation across a community.

THE CORE TASK OF LEADERSHIP: REFORMING OR RECHARGING?

The external pressures on public schools to change are obvious to anyone. National commissions have pronounced a crisis and suggested several remedies. State governors and legislators seem compelled to demonstrate that they are doing something to improve education—through career ladders, improvement plans, or leadership academies. Less obvious to school principals, district superintendents, and some academics is exactly what these external constituencies want. Legislators seem fairly clear: they want schools restructured. But are these desires echoed at the local level? Do parents and communities want schools to change? Or do interested local groups want schools to change back? Do they want schools reformed, or do they want them renewed? What people want at the local level is less clear. The local ambiguity, coupled with seeming certainty at state and federal levels, creates a fundamental dilemma for educational leadership. If the prevailing ways and practices of schools need changing, then existing cultural patterns make the going extremely rough— as past experience has reaffirmed again and again. If, however, the resilient culture of schools needs reviewing and renewing, then the common interest in education provides an interesting opportunity—if we can only figure out what to do.

Dilemmas, by their nature, are insoluble. The meaning of any enterprise is anchored on symbols, and change produces ambiguity and loss. Worn-out symbols undermine meaning and stimulate hopeful searches for alternatives. Schools now undoubtedly suffer from the residual effects of two decades of innovative improvement and reform. While still reeling from the last efforts to make things different, teachers and principals are again being confronted with demands for more change. They are encouraged to try something new while they still grapple with what they have lost.

Managers solve problems. Leaders confront dilemmas. Leaders reframe impossible dilemmas into novel opportunities. Leaders in organizations across all sectors are confronted with many of the same issues that educators now face: (1) How do we encourage meaning and commitment? (2) How do we deal with loss and change? and (3) How can we shape symbols that convey the essence of the enterprise to insiders and outsiders? Educational leaders must create artful ways to reweave organizational tapestries from old traditions, current realities, and future visions. This work cannot be done by clinging to old ways, emulating principles from effective schools and excellent companies, or divining futuristic images from what we imagine the next decades will be like. Rather, it takes a collective look backward, inward, and ahead—in education on the part of administrators, teachers, parents, students, and other members of a school community. It is a process of transformation akin to the one that produces a butterfly from a caterpillar—a cocoon of human experience in which past, present, and future are fused together in an organic process.

How can a leader move from the metaphoric to a literal course of action? I typically respond to corporate leaders who ask this question, "It will come to you—probably through a time of creative brooding that involves others in the company." This charge produces a bewildered first response, followed in time by some highly creative strategies. Here are some examples from education to create a yeasty foment for reforming while revitalizing the culture of public schools:

1. *Recreate the history of a school.* In New York City, several elementary schools convened groups of parents, teachers, administrators, students, alumni, and retirees in sessions to build the story of a particular school. From the deliberations, people came to see their roots and realities. In all cases, the juxtaposition of past and present created a shared sense of new direction—a shared vision for the school. In the aggregate, these schools showed dramatic improvements in test scores, attendance, vandalism rates, and other measures of school performance.

2. *Articulate shared values.* What a school "stands for" needs to be shared. In top-quality companies, slogans provide a shorthand that makes essential characteristics accessible. Symbols, rituals, and artifacts represent intangible values. One school district, along with a local advertising group, recently made a commercial for its school. The intended audience was twofold (as it is in any advertisement): consumers and workers. The response to the commercials was overwhelmingly positive. Efforts of teachers and students have been reinforced and shared.

3. *Anoint and celebrate heroes.* Every school has a pantheon of heroes—past, present, and future. Their annointment and celebration provide tangible human examples of shared values and beliefs. A

recent call to my office from the new principal of my old high school offers a novel example:

"We would like you to visit your alma mater," the principal said.

"Why?" I responded.

"Because you have done all right for yourself," she said, "and from all indicators you weren't supposed to. Your teachers remember you as particularly troublesome. Your classmates recall exploits of mischief rather than demonstrations of academic worth. The records reveal a grade-point average that is, at best, unimpressive. The assistant principal notes that you spent more time in her office and the halls than you did in class. Your football coach was certain you'd end up in prison. In short, we want you on campus to show other trouble-makers that there may be hope for them."

Countless other similar opportunities to celebrate teachers, students, administrators, or parents who exemplify intangible values exist in every school.

4. *Reinvigorate rituals and ceremonies.* Rituals and ceremonies provide regular and special occasions for learning, celebrating, and binding individuals to traditions and values. The parents of a public high school recently gave a banquet for its teachers. Teachers arrived at the school's cafeteria, greeted by corsages and ribbons labeled with terms such as guru, mentor, or exemplar. The cafeteria tables were draped with white linen tablecloths and bedecked with silver candelabra with lighted candles. Teachers and parents sang together at a piano, drinking wine and eating cheese. The dinner was potluck; each parent brought a dish. The program, following dinner, called attention to the history, values, and vision of the school. The school choir sang. The event delighted the entire audience—and transformed the school.

The principal of a large high school required his faculty to attend the annual graduation ceremony and wear their academic robes. If requested, the district paid the rental fee. Parents and students received the graduation ceremony with acclaim. The next year, attendance at the event doubled. Drinking and other discipline problems have disappeared. Parent confidence in the school has gone up dramatically.

5. *Tell good stories.* At a recent junior high school faculty meeting, teachers spent the time telling stories about students and each other. As a result, several exemplary students were identified, one a student

who had changed from a troublemaker to a top student nearly overnight. In doing so, he overcame nearly insurmountable family and learning problems. The faculty thus convened an awards assembly to recognize all the exemplary students and share their stories with the other students. The most dramatically improved student was awarded a large brass eagle. The award now carries the student's name and is given each year to the one who improves the most.

6. *Work with the informal network of cultural players.* A collection of priests, gossips, and storytellers presides over each school's culture. Often, those roles are occupied by nonprofessionals such as secretaries, food service workers, or custodians. Such people provide important linkages inside and are often a direct conduit to the local community. These people need encouragement. They need recognition. One school named a new patio after a custodian, a man who served an important role as a keeper of the history of the school, conveying to both teachers and students the rich legacy of past exploits and glories. When changes are proposed, the informal network must be intimately involved. Otherwise, these people will sabotage the effort.

USING OUTSIDE PRESSURE TO BUILD FROM WITHIN

The effective-schools movement and state reform initiatives create external pressures often interpreted as a need to significantly change the culture of public schools. At times, such alternatives may be needed. But rather than following the prescriptions suggested or imposed by others, schools need to look inside themselves, both historically and contemporarily.

Old practices and other losses need to be buried and commemorated. Meaningless practices and symbols need to be analyzed and revitalized. Emerging visions, dreams, and hopes need to be articulated and celebrated. These are the core tasks that will occupy educational leaders for several years to come.

REFERENCES

Baldridge, J. Victor. "Organizational Change: Institutional Sagas, External Challenges, and Internal Politics." In *Managing Change in Educational Organizations*, edited by J. Victor Baldridge and Terrence E. Deal, pp. 427–448. Berkeley: McCutchan, 1975.

Baldridge, J. Victor, and Deal, Terrence E. *The Dynamics of Organizational Change in Education*. Berkeley: McCutchan, 1983.

Bolman, Lee G., and Deal, Terrence E. *Modern Approaches to Understanding and Managing Organizations*. San Francisco: Jossey-Bass, 1984.

Clark, Burton R. "The Organizational Saga in Higher Education." In *Managing Change in Educational Organizations*, edited by J. Victor Baldridge and Terrence E. Deal, pp. 98–108. Berkeley: McCutchan, 1975.

Coleman, James S. *Equality of Educational Opportunity*. Washington D.C.: U.S. Government Printing Office, 1966.

Corwin, Ronald G. "Strategies for Organizational Innovation: An Empirical Comparison," *American Sociological Review* 37 (1972): 441–452.

Deal, Terrence E. "Symbolism of Effective Schools," *Elementary School Journal* 85 (January 1985a): 3.

Deal, Terrence E. "National Commissions: Blueprints for Remodeling," *Education and Urban Society* 17 (February 1985b): 2

Deal, Terrence, and Kennedy, Allan. *Corporate Cultures: The Rites and Rituals of Corporate Life*. Reading, Mass.: Addison-Wesley, 1982.

Halpin, Andrew W., and Croft, D. B. *The Organizational Climate of Schools*. St. Louis, Mo.: Washington University, 1962.

Marris, P. *Loss and Change*. London: Routledge & Kegan Paul, 1974.

McDill, Edward, and Rigsby, Leo C. *Structure and Process in Secondary Schools*. Baltimore: John Hopkins University Press, 1973.

McPherson, Gertrude. *Small Town Teacher*. Cambridge, Mass.: Harvard University Press, 1972.

Meyer, John, and Rowan, Brian. "The Structure of Educational Organizations." In *The Dynamics of Organizational Change in Education*, edited by J. Victor Baldridge and Terrence E. Deal. Berkeley: McCutchan, 1983.

Peters, T. J., and Waterman, R. H., Jr. *In Search of Excellence*. New York: Harper & Row, 1982.

Rutter, Michael; Maugham, Barbara; Mortimore, Peter; Ouston, Janet; and Smith, Alan. *Fifteen Thousand Hours: Secondary Schools and Their Effects on Children*. Cambridge, Mass.: Harvard University Press, 1979.

Sarason, Seymour. *The Culture of the School and the Problem of Change*. Boston: Allyn and Bacon, 1971.

Swidler, Ann. *Organization Without Authority*. Cambridge, Mass.: Harvard University Press, 1979.

Waller, Willard. *The Sociology of Teaching*. New York: Wiley, 1932.

Chapter 2

BUREAUCRATIC AND CULTURAL LINKAGES: IMPLICATIONS FOR THE PRINCIPAL

William A. Firestone and Bruce L. Wilson

How much do principals influence instruction in their schools? There are two contradictory images. The first is of the principal as instructional leader, a powerful individual with great potential to improve teachers' performance. The second is of the principal isolated from teachers who barricade themselves behind classroom doors. Both images are oversimplifications. To understand how principals (and others) can influence educational practice and use the most effective strategies, one must move beyond the formal authority of office to examine the wide array of linkage mechanisms that connect principals to teachers.

Linkages coordinate the activity of people who work in schools, and the principal has quite a variety of linkages available. Some rely on the formal bureaucracy, while others work through the school's culture. Although each linkage by itself tends to be very loose, with limited influence over teacher activity, the pattern of linkages can tightly constrain what teachers do. To influence teachers, principals must understand the pattern of linkages in their school and use it in a coordinated way.

We first describe the concept of linkage in schools and the distinction between bureaucratic and cultural linkages. Next, we discuss how principals can work with bureaucratic and cultural linkages. Bureaucratic linkages create or limit opportunities for certain kinds of

19

action. They can be modified through formal decisions. Cultural linkages affect the way teachers (and students) think about their work. Such linkages are changed by the principal's symbolic activity, and sometimes the same activity can have implications for both bureaucratic and cultural linkages. In the third section we assess the problems of using linkages to change instruction and suggest that the challenge is to coordinate many small actions as much as it is to make a few dramatic ones. Finally we point out that linkages are also affected by factors outside the school. We suggest how the state can affect bureaucratic linkages through its testing policy, and we use the recent history of reform commission reports as an example of changing cultural linkages.

SCHOOL LINKAGES

Linkages coordinate the actions of individuals in organizations. They are tight when the activity of person A leads to some kind of activity by person B. Here linkage implies responsiveness. Such linkages come about through communication, persuasion, the use of rewards and punishments, or simply the passing of a part down an assembly line. They are short term and direct. In other situations linkage implies predictability. That is, person A pretty well knows that person B will behave in a certain way. Schedules, rules, norms, values, and goals all promote this kind of linkage. In these cases the time between the action and the linked response may be extended and the connection may be less direct, but the response may be more persistent.

In comparison to other organizations, schools are loosely linked. While there is some disagreement about what the full range of linkage mechanisms is, most observers focus on the lack of strong bureaucratic ties, especially through the weak formal hierarchy in schools. Researchers describe how instruction is uncoupled from the formal line of authority running from the superintendent to the classroom. They talk about the isolation of teachers from both superiors and colleagues. Researchers have contrasted the control exercised by teachers within the classroom with how little they have outside the classroom (Bidwell, 1965; Weick, 1976).

Bureaucratic and Cultural Linkages

The concept of linkage not only highlights the looseness of each specific mechanism but also the variety of ways that are available to integrate and coordinate activity in schools. To understand the variety of linkages, it is necessary to look at both the bureaucratic and the cultural sides of schools.

Bureaucratic linkages are the formal, enduring arrangements that allow an organization to operate. These include the roles, and rules, procedures, and authority relations that prescribe the school's framework, the things found in a teachers' handbook, or board policy. These linkages control the behavior of teachers, students, administrators, and all others in the school. However, the prescribed framework alone gives a limited, static picture of the school. It must be renegotiated periodically. It is often violated, sometimes for the school's own good; and it is intentionally re-created on occasion through reorganizations that cannot be understood simply with reference to the formal organizational chart.

Activity in school is also patterned by its culture. Culture refers to the subjective side of the organization. More specifically, a culture is the system of publicly accepted meanings for the activities of a group of people. Analysis of organizational culture focuses on its content (that is, the meanings that are shared); on the means of denoting the culture through symbols, stories, and rituals; and on how people communicate the cultural meanings that they share. Business researchers recently have discussed the importance of organizational cultures to the success of a business, finding that culture can be an important linkage mechanism in business environments. Likewise, an organizational culture can be the glue that holds a school together, but subcultures can create problems for internal coordination (Deal and Kennedy, 1982; Peters and Waterman, 1982).

Because cultures arise naturally in organizations, a principal may not think of them as a linkage mechanism to improve instruction. However, one view of the manager's leadership responsibility is to create coherence between the organization's basic purposes and its culture. Strong cultures with appropriate content can promote school effectiveness, and principals can contribute to such cultures.

Two school characteristics make it hard to create strong cultures in schools. First, the basic purposes of schools are ambiguous, poorly specified, and much debated. Schools have too many purposes that are hard to prioritize, so it is difficult to develop a culture with a clear focus. Second, teachers are isolated, not only from administrators, but also from each other. They get most of their work satisfaction from students rather than peers. For that reason it is hard for teachers to develop a strong, binding culture. Thus, cultural linkages, like bureaucratic ones, will be weak in schools. Still, the principal can influence both bureaucratic and cultural linkages and use the combination to improve instruction.

LINKAGES, INSTRUCTION, AND THE PRINCIPAL

Bureaucratic and cultural linkages work in different ways. Bureaucratic linkages establish constraints and opportunities for teachers. Cultural linkages shape what teachers want to do or how they take advantage of those constraints. Both make teacher behavior more predictable. They can also affect what students learn directly. In the next two sections we examine how each kind of linkage relates to instruction and how each can be manipulated. Principals face a further difficulty because the same action can affect bureaucratic and cultural linkages differently. The third section illustrates this point.

Bureaucratic Linkages

Bureaucratic linkage mechanisms include formal supervision, rules and procedures, plans and schedules, and information systems that include attendance reporting, grades, and tests. Principals are commonly thought to affect instruction primarily through supervision and evaluation. Supervision is attractive because it seems so direct: one person helps or directs another person to do something. There is, as a result, a strong belief that principals ought to supervise assertively. Many professional associations, state education agencies, and administrator training programs are now developing ways to tighten the supervisory linkage.

Yet, past experience suggests that while supervision can be improved, it will not become the master linkage through which principals massively change teaching. For supervision to be effective, it must be done frequently; more is better. Yet, principals do not supervise often. The formal cycle of preconference, formal observation, and postconference is rarely repeated. Even when money is on the line in merit pay programs, any given teacher may be supervised only three or four times a year. Under normal circumstances, with experienced teachers, principals supervise even less often. For supervision to be effective, recommendations in an evaluation must be followed up. Just pointing out weaknesses creates insecurity and resentment. Time must be committed to follow-up activities that will help teachers overcome weaknesses. Supervision is ineffective because each principal is responsible for too many teachers, there are too many other competing responsibilities, and there are too few incentives for principals to devote adequate energy to the task. Supervision is even harder in secondary schools where content specialization means that principals may lack the expertise to adequately evaluate performance and where teachers question their authority to do so.

If the effectiveness of supervision has been overrated, other linkages that indirectly influence teachers' behavior are often underrated. The principal has considerable influence over several key work structures. By altering these structures, principals can influence how teachers interact with one another and feel about their work. Here are five examples of such linkages along with ways principals can influence them to improve instruction.

First, the principal has substantial influence over the amount of time students spend on academic tasks. The principal can make a powerful impact by protecting classrooms from external interruptions and altering activities to maximize instructional time. One strategy is to guard prime instructional time zealously. The principal at Garden Hills School in Atlanta, Georgia, makes this point when he says, "[This] school holds sacred an uninterrupted basic skills time block each morning. The time from 9:00 to 10:30 cannot be interrupted." Another way to increase time is to ease noninstructional duties for teachers. The principal at Laura B. Sprague School in Lincolnshire, Illinois, has organized the schedule so that teachers have no responsibility for lunch money collection, study hall, or other duties that "would keep them away from their primary task of educating children."* These bureaucratic linkages help establish that academic learning time is critical.

---

*Unless otherwise noted, specific examples given in this chapter are drawn from schools recognized by the U.S. Department of Education for their unusually successful programs and practices. Further documentation on these, as well as other examples, can be found in Wilson and Corcoran (1987, 1989).

Second, class size and the grouping of students influence the delivery of instruction. By controlling the number of children in a particular room and the mix of gender, race, or ages, the principal can influence the quality of instruction and ultimately student achievement. Shaker Heights High School near Cleveland offers a useful example. In the last two decades the proportion of black students in this school increased from 8 to 40 percent. Academic excellence has always been a hallmark of the school; the challenge was to continue that excellence with a changing student population. The first response was to create a tracking system that produced de facto segregation and a negative reaction from the black community. Using ideas from the community, the school implemented a number of new recommendations and garnered support for improvements. As the principal observed, "The issue is on everyone's agenda, and there is a genuine concern about doing better. We have accepted it as our problem, one that we are willing to struggle with until we find some answers."

Third, principals can also influence the working patterns of teachers by arranging physical space and free time to promote norms of collegiality and experimentation, both of which have been associated with school effectiveness. Promoting collegiality is well illustrated by Northfield Elementary School in Ellicott City, Maryland. The school works hard to ensure that teachers assigned to the same grade level have joint planning periods to encourage collaboration, to set aside meeting time to share in-service experiences, and to structure opportunities for teachers to observe each other's work.

Fourth, principals often have some discretionary resources (money, released time, materials) at their disposal and, through their judicious distribution, can greatly enhance innovative instructional activities. Discretionary resources are often associated with wealthy communities. However, the staff at Byng High School in Ada, Oklahoma—a poor school with almost half the students from low-income families—have improvised with real creativity. By using donated land, stockpiling building materials when a favorable price appeared, and having construction done by vocational students and maintenance staff, they have created a masterpiece facility. But more important than the physical plant is the pride engendered by the whole school's involvement. As one observer noted, "The teachers don't think of themselves as resourceful." In creating such an image, they have created a climate conducive to learning.

Finally, knowledge and skills are another area where linkages can be tightened. Principals can encourage the use of previously unused or underused skills within a classroom as well as networking those skills among teachers. The principal can also encourage teachers to seek new knowledge and facilitate that activity by recommending training sessions and providing resources for attendance. While in-service activity is an obvious vehicle to develop knowledge and skills, staff at many schools seem to be simply going through the motions— attending meetings but retaining or using little of the presented material. The principal at Eakin School in Nashville, Tennessee, has actively involved teachers in planning these activites to tighten this linkage. A teacher committee at Eakin conducts a needs assessment for in-service activities, sets priorities, plans programs, secures consultants, and evaluates program success.

Less attention may be given to the principal's contribution in these areas because control is often shared with district administrators and supervisors. In a few districts, however, site-based management gives the principal (sometimes in conjunction with teachers) considerable control over these plans. In either case, an integrated approach that attends to both supervisory and planning mechanisms will have a greater impact on instruction than any effort that attends to only one of those areas.

Cultural Linkages

While bureaucratic linkages coordinate action formally, cultural linkages directly influence how people think about what they do. Cultural linkages affect at least two aspects of thought. The first is the individual's definitions of the task. The school's organizational culture provides answers to such questions as: What does it mean to teach? What techniques or approaches are available? What are the children like who are being taught? What are the outcomes of the teaching process? The second is the individual's commitment to the task. Commitment refers to the individual's willingness to devote energy and loyalty to the organization and the attachment of that person to the organization. It includes a willingness to stay at a school, emotional ties to the school, and voluntary agreement to conform to local rules and norms.

Task definitions are important because there are few clear

answers to questions about what is to be done or how to do it in schools. Moreover, teachers' expectations for students directly affect what is learned. Commitment is an issue because education is a low-commitment occupation where people often have strong conflicting attachments to family or other jobs, especially at the secondary level. Often, the improvement of instruction requires more effort as well as a different kind of effort.

For the principal, a focus on cultural linkages raises three questions:

- What cultural content promotes successful instruction? (What task definitions and commitments are preferable?)
- How is that culture denoted? (What forms, symbols, or stories carry the desired content?)
- How and to what extent can the principal influence the school's culture?

Cultural Content. The appropriate culture for successful instruction can be derived from a number of sources. One source is the culture of successful institutions. Here it is important to be clear about what "successful" means. For instance, a study of especially innovative school districts identified similar cultures that emphasized diversity in services delivered, improving educational service rather than "bureaucratic or political" concerns, open boundaries to the environment to help teachers learn about new approaches and new resources, and mutual trust and encouragement for risk taking (Berman and McLaughlin, 1979). Successful large corporations have similar cultures that stress trying things rather than doing elaborate planning, staying close to customers and trying out new ideas on them, individual autonomy and entrepreneurship, a belief that productivity comes through people, strong definitions of what the company stands for and the kinds of products in which it deals, and a commitment to developing high-quality products. The effective-schools literature suggested an emphasis on basic skills (many would now include higher-order thinking as well), high expectations for all students, and an orderly environment. All this research suggests that a culture that improves instruction provides a very clear image of what a successful student is like and makes that more important than anything else. Other cultural elements that help include a commitment to quality service, a willingness to take risks, and close ties to the outside world, which is a source of ideas as well as of political and financial support.

The study of successful institutions in other spheres helps address the problem of commitment and that part of the task definition issue related to how people should interact with each other. It does not address the more central issue of task definition, however, which is to define the craft of effective teaching. Advances in this area can be made partly by synthesizing the existing research on teaching and deriving from it some themes that one might hope to find in the professional culture of schools. However, it may be necessary for politicians and the public to get a clearer view about the relative importance of basic skills versus higher-order thinking, whether all students are expected to succeed, and which of the many things schools endeavor to teach are really important.

Cultural Denotation. The study of cultures frequently separates the contents of a culture from its expressions. The latter refer to the ways an organization communicates those contents to its members. Typically, the major themes in a culture are expressed redundantly through a variety of symbol systems. In fact, it is from the repetitions of a theme that a positive effect results and people begin to share ways of thinking. Understanding how symbols work is complex because effective symbols are inherently ambiguous. The power of symbols comes from the way they combine particular elements of the specific situation with more general, powerful issues or concerns of all humankind. Moreover, the relationship among these special and general elements may shift with the situation, and the most powerful symbols may combine a number of such elements.

Three symbol systems communicate the contents of an organization's culture: stories, icons, and rituals. Stories include myths and legends as well as true events. The true event takes on much of its meaning as it is interpreted in the telling. Usually stories are about individuals and are interpreted to indicate positively or negatively valued traits of the likely consequences of certain actions. They are often about heroes, but who a hero is may vary. Sometimes it is a now mythical figure like the founder of a company (e.g., Thomas Watson of IBM) or the person who gives a school a new mission (e.g., Debbie Meier of Central Park East in New York). At other times it is one of "the common workers," like the assembly-line worker who made the company president put on safety glasses while touring her area. Stories have been collected in both business and higher education settings, but not to the same extent in schools. It would be useful to find out what stories circulate among school teachers (and students).

Icons and rituals also communicate culture. Icons are the physical manifestations (logos, mottoes, and trophies) while rituals are ceremonial activities. A great deal can be learned about schools through analyses of assemblies, teachers' meetings, community functions, report cards, awards and trophies, lesson plans, and the furnishing of classrooms and work spaces among other things. For instance, what does it say about school cultures that athletes wear letter sweaters but straight A students (or speech and debate stars, or science fair winners) do not?

In addition to symbol systems, the study of cultures must examine communication patterns. Stories and symbols carry their meaning through an ongoing flow of communications among organizational members. While opportunities to share are more limited in schools than in other organizations, it would still be useful to understand more about how informal networks work. Do schools have the same kinds of priests, whisperers, gossips, found in business? How central is the school secretary to communication and with whom? Do people who "hang out" regularly in the teachers' lounge play a different role from those who stay in their department offices or their own classrooms?

Culture and the Principal. The third question about cultural linkages is, How does the principal influence them? While the current management literature is rather optimistic about the ability of managers to shape cultures, there are others who believe that an organization's culture develops incrementally and largely outside anyone's conscious control. It is probably too soon to know how susceptible schools' professional cultures are to administrative influence. Nonetheless, we have a number of ideas about how principals can influence the culture of their schools.

First, principals can manage the flow of stories and other information in their schools. For instance, in the 1960s when there was frequent disorder in many schools, observers viewed the problem as a collective protest. One principal, Mr. Brandt, maintained an orderly school by defining problems as rare individual outbursts that teachers could handle with patience and skills. He frequently told stories such as the following that reinforced his own view:

I saw this done beautifully in a classroom with the kids. "I ain't going to study today, 'cause I don't feel like it." And the teacher just grinned at him. And she said, "Well, I'm going to give you a book just in case you change your mind." In five minutes he was studying. [Metz, 1978, pp. 195–196]

Rituals are a second way to communicate the school's culture. These repeated ceremonial activities include assemblies, teacher meetings, and parent-teacher conferences. A principal can also create and shape rituals. By placing priority on academic assemblies or rewards for especially effective teachers, the principal can help shape preferred behaviors. In some cases the principal may actually become a symbol. The principal's own deportment can symbolize to the adults and students in the school a new order where education is taken more seriously.

Terrence Deal has written about a powerful ritual at Concord High School in Massachusetts, where parents hosted a celebration in honor of teachers. He described the scene as follows:

They decorated the cafeteria and put silver candle holders on tables covered with white linen. Each teacher received a corsage on arrival bearing the terms guru, mentor, guide, and teacher. Parents and teachers sang songs together around a piano bar. . . . Dinner was potluck; each parent brought a dish. After dinner, speeches and choral music from students completed the evening. [Deal, 1985, p. 617]

This represents a forceful ritual ceremony that helped build a sense of identity and commitment to the school.

Another equally important aspect of communicating the culture of the school comes from the specialized, informal communication roles that facilitate the transfer of stories and the operation of rituals. Stories and rituals build meaning through the ongoing flow of communication that ensures appropriate interpretation of the messages. While a variety of people may fill those communication roles, the principal can structure situations to maximize the exposure of key storytellers.

A creative example of the use of storytellers comes from Barrington Elementary School in Upper Arlington, Ohio. The school has created a buddy system that matches new parents in the community with "old-timers." The old-timers serve to communicate a sense of the school to the uninitiated. They establish a positive link with the newcomers that builds ownership and pride in the school. The old-timers also serve as a useful recruiting device to get people to attend and volunteer for important ceremonies and rituals in the school.

Finally, principals can also serve as central communicators of the culture. Anyone with the day-to-day experience of being a principal is acutely aware of the multiple impromptu opportunities to interact with teachers and students. Principals are constantly "wandering around" the school, a highly praised business management technique. By introducing more consistency across these hundreds of interactions, principals can use them to improve the culture for instruction.

An excellent example of how the power to communicate can influence a school comes from our field notes while we were working in the mid-1980s with the John Bartram High School in Philadelphia. At the time the school had over 3,600 students and 265 professional staff. The principal could not communicate directly with everyone each day. However, he used three strategies to communicate effectively with his staff. First, he employed an active cabinet of vice-principals and department heads. All important issues were discussed in that group before the principal made a decision. Second, teachers could raise issues with their department heads, who then brought them up in cabinet meetings. Finally, the principal turned an office on the top floor of the school into a lounge. Periodically, he announced that he would be in that room. Teachers were free to come to him to raise issues. This was done in addition to having an open-door policy where teachers could approach him with a variety of concerns.

Simultaneous Effects of Principal Action

Although bureaucratic and cultural linkages are conceptually distinct, a principal may influence both at once. This can work for the principal if effects on both linkages are complementary, but it will be counterproductive if those effects are contradictory. A few examples will illustrate this issue. Consider first ability grouping. Grouping to minimize variation in ability allows classes with faster students to move more quickly through the curriculum and get to enrichment material or address more complex topics while classes with less intelligent students proceed more slowly and cover material more intensively until students learn the material. Thus, from a pure management perspective, there seems to be some advantage to ability grouping. Yet, grouping also labels students and creates differential expectations for what they will learn. Lowered teacher expectations (a part of the school culture) will seriously impair the education of less able students.

Discipline policies are another example. They can help maintain order, which increases time for instruction. Such policies will limit opportunities for higher-order cognitive thinking and more advanced social development, however, if they are administered in a way that views the child as an empty vessel who has no ideas and must follow adult rules. If the same discipline policies are grounded in a more developmental view that sees students as active learners, more opportunities for advanced learning will occur. At the most authoritarian extreme, excessive emphasis on discipline and order can actually create a culture that impairs learning. Thus, the same bureaucratic linkage can have very different impacts depending on the cultural meaning imposed on it. As these examples indicate, an important task for the principal is to ensure that bureaucratic and cultural linkages are mutually reinforcing.

Bureaucratic linkages can also reinforce cultural content as sometimes happens with resource allocation. Allocation of discretionary funds in a fair manner that provides extensive support for instruction can promote commitment among teachers and signal that teaching and learning are more important than political or bureaucratic concerns.

THE PROBLEMS OF WORKING THROUGH LINKAGES

Neither school culture nor bureaucratic linkages alone are powerful means to influence instruction. The principal's contribution comes through the orchestration of a variety of actions working through an array of linkages to have a consistent impact on what is taught and how. Why this is so becomes apparent when one considers the separate effects of a principal's efforts to use each linkage mechanism as a means of improving instruction.

One difficulty with employing bureaucratic linkages is that the principal's influence over them is constrained. Teacher autonomy limits the utility of supervision. The effectiveness of plans is constrained in two ways. First, principals' options are severely restricted by external policies. The major design decisions about school programs have been in place since early in this century and are codified in state law or board policy. The principal may have some say at the margins over whether the school day has six periods or seven. However, more basic decisions about whether there will be a counseling department, a sports program, or a social studies department are already decided. Similarly, curriculum and grouping decisions are often constrained by district policies, disciplinary actions by court decisions, and the distribution of discretionary resources by the fact that those resources are quite small when compared to the overall budget of the school, most of which is committed to personnel.

Second, even when the principal makes a decision, she rarely makes it alone. The principal's role is highly interactive, requiring discussions with teachers, district office staff, and—in high schools—department heads. The nature of this interaction is not so clear, however; some people stress the reactive nature of the principal's role and others the proactive. Still, major decisions are often delegated, made by committees, or guided by formulas in ways that limit the principal's discretion to shape teaching conditions.

What conditions increase the principal's opportunities to shape the bureaucratic linkages governing teachers? One is the opportunity to thoroughly rethink the bureaucratic structure of the school, which is being made possible by the current restructuring movement. Organizations like the Coalition of Essential Schools encourage schools to rethink their basic curriculum and the division of labor needed to operate it. Some states are making it much easier to get waivers from regulations than was formerly the case. Often, however, these changes are supposed to include a significant increase in teacher participation in decisions that adjust bureaucratic linkages. Thus, restructuring creates an unusual opportunity to rearrange bureaucratic linkages, but the principal must often influence others in the process.

So far, however, for all the publicity attached to restructuring, few schools are making radical changes. Within the current system then, how well the principal uses bureaucratic linkages may depend on that person's own assertiveness. Even though a decision must be made at the district level, the principal can offer input and advice. It is usually unwise to assume that one has no influence because one's authority is limited. Moreover, the principal who consults with people about decisions that she must make can use those opportunities to persuade others to a particular point of view as well as collect information.

The greatest opportunity for the principal to influence bureaucratic linkages actually comes from the ambiguity surrounding both that role and the organization of the school. Formal policies often need to be clarified and are sometimes contradictory. By interpreting policy, the principal gains authority to shape instruction. For instance, one principal used a little known state law to buttress a decision on pledge of allegiance ceremonies when district policies were going against him. He even sought support from the local district attorney when his interpretation was challenged.

The use of cultural linkages to shape instruction depends on another kind of ambiguity—that governing the principal-teacher relationship. Teachers are ambivalent about principals. On the one hand they want to be left alone, free from the principal's direction and interference. On the other hand they want concern and appreciation, a word of praise after spending almost all their working day with no adult contact. They also look to their principal for certain kinds of support: a safe, orderly school environment, help with discipline problems, and protection from parents and community groups who challenge their decisions. Usually, they do not see that their wants may require a trade-off; they want it all.

This ambiguity stems from three characteristics of teaching. First, neither criteria for success nor means of achieving it are clear. Even when the results come out right, teachers find it hard to know if they can take credit. This ambiguity leads to the second characteristic: vulnerability. Teachers are sensitive to infringements on their authority and autonomy from both the public and students. Finally, teaching is a lonely occupation with little chance to talk about one's work with others who can appreciate what one has done.

Because of these conditions, many teachers want to view the principal as a powerful, wise individual whose praise is meaningful and protection is sure. The principal is in the right place to become a reference point and to establish norms because she is close, has relevant expertise, and is in a position of authority. As a result, teachers invest a good deal of affect in their view of the principal; the office is a symbolic one that can be used to manipulate the stories and rituals that interpret teachers' work. On the other hand, when the principal cannot meet teachers' standards, when things go wrong that no one can control, there is a strong tendency to scapegoat and blame the principal. This too is a cultural process, one that can victimize the principal rather than being used to advantage.

Although principals are well placed to affect the school's culture, it is not clear how well that culture can influence instruction. Often when a principal "turns around" a school, the change is in student climate and discipline. Instruction can remain unchanged. It is not clear if principals' impact is limited because they have more control over discipline or because they do not try to shape instructional practice. In many schools principals seem overly ready to leave instruction to teachers without trying to shape thinking about instructional content or process. Thus, even though results have been less than impressive in the past, the potential for influence may be there but unrealized.

In sum, no single linkage will provide a magic wand to give the principal great influence over the school's instructional program. Rather, the principal has a number of weak means of control or coordination available. These are employed through countless interactions with teachers over the course of the school day and year. A few interactions result in strategic decisions affecting major time and resource allocations (bureaucratic linkages) or the school's culture, but most are quite minor. These interactions can become so numerous that the principal is more reactive than proactive. The principal's task is to develop a clear vision of the purposes of the school that gives primacy to instruction and to carry that vision through consistently during those countless interactions. By doing so, the principal uses bureaucratic linkages to create opportunities for teachers to follow that vision and minimizes chances to operate in different ways. At the same time, the principal uses cultural linkages to communicate that vision so that, to a greater or lesser extent, it becomes the teachers' own culture. The initiative for carrying out instructional work then rests with teachers, but they are much more likely to incorporate the principal's perspective.

LINKAGES AND THE OUTSIDE WORLD

When thinking about school leadership, there is a tendency to take existing linkages as given and forget where they come from. The school is thus viewed as a system isolated from the world around it. In fact, linkages result from the larger political-cultural world in which schools are found. As that world changes, so do the linkages. Changing linkages can create new opportunities but also new challenges for the principal. Two recent examples of external pressure illustrate how these changes affect the principal and efforts to improve teaching and learning. The bureaucratic example is the increasing role of testing. The cultural example is the use of commission reports in the 1980s as a reform symbol.

Testing as a Bureaucratic Linkage

Tests may be the ultimate bureaucratic linkage mechanism. As part of the information management system of the school or the state, they provide a measure of outputs, of how well schools are achieving their mission to educate children. They can serve their control and coordination functions in a variety of ways. Sometimes they just provide information on the performance of schools, districts, groups of students, or the nation. Some states administer tests to help parents and educators understand how a particular school compares with others in the state. The reporting of annual averages on the Scholastic Achievement Test (SAT) or state scores on the new National Assessment of Educational Progress works the same way. It has become more common to make tests high-stakes instruments for the distribution of rewards and sometimes punishments. Some states and districts mandate that students must pass a particular test to be promoted to the next grade or to graduate from high school. Others allocate funds to schools and teachers from test results. Even when tests are not formally used to distribute funds, they can have a similar effect. District test scores sometimes effect bond issue elections and votes on tax levies. The introduction of high-stakes tests is fairly recent. Their function as a graduation requirement began in the 1970s. When important stakes are attached, tests have a great deal of impact on instruction. The early high school graduation tests focused on basic skills. They ensured that all students were introduced to those skills and spent more time practicing them, but they also directed attention away from subjects and capacities that were not tested. High-stakes tests are a linkage that effectively limits teacher autonomy and makes their behavior more predictable. Teachers report that such tests reduce the use of their own professional judgment, increase the de-

mands on how they use their time, and create more pressure for
higher scores.

The principal lacks control over the crucial factors that determine
the meaning of testing policies, such as state decisions about a test's
content and the stakes attached to it. However, the principal can
influence other factors to a greater or lesser degree. Some are decided
at the district level so that the principal has a chance to persuade
others to a particular course of action. Others are services that the
principal can lobby for or arrange to get through alternative sources
(e.g., a school secretary rather than someone in the central office).
Still others really can happen in the building. Here are a few examples:

1. *Alignment between test and curriculum.* The overlap between a
   particular general achievement test and school curriculum is
   often as low as 50 percent. When overlap is low, teachers may
   not view the test as a legitimate measure of student performance. They may either ignore the test or teach to it by
   helping students cram just before its administration. When
   alignment is high, teachers can spread test preparation over a
   longer period of time, and it becomes part of their regular
   work.
2. *Rapidity and comprehensibility of feedback.* When teachers get the
   results back quickly, they are more likely to use the data for
   systematic planning. The same is true when data are provided
   in a form that is easy to understand.
3. *Symbolic interpretation of tests.* When the principal spends time
   discussing test results with teachers, displays results, and
   announces them, teachers will take them seriously. The quality
   of that seriousness depends on the interpretation the principal
   puts on them. The principal can define a test as an external
   means of control over individual teachers or the school as a
   whole by suggesting that dire consequences will result from
   low scores. Then teachers will take drastic measures like
   teaching to the test or even cheating. The principal can also
   define a test as a useful source of information for an individual
   or a building through joint planning that helps teachers use
   tests to identify strengths and areas for improvement. The
   principal can also help teachers employ tests to develop action

plans, curriculum revisions, and the like. Then teachers are more likely to use tests as data sources for improvement.

Commission Reports and Cultural Linkages

The 1980s were notable in part for the number of educational reform commissions that formed. Right around 1983 as many as sixteen national commissions and 175 state task forces issued reports calling for educational reforms. The most notable of these was *A Nation at Risk* (National Commission on Excellence in Education, 1983). Three years later at least five more prestigious commissions issued reports. If one views these reports as an instrumental means to change policy (bureaucratic linkages), the results were disappointing. The quantity and the drama of the rhetoric exceeded the number of new policies enacted, and the new policies exceeded the amount of change observed in schools. If, however, one views these same reports as a symbolic activity to reaffirm and build the culture of schools, the results were more positive.

The reform reports stem from the changes of the 1960s. In many schools those changes tore the fabric of the existing school culture. The authority of teachers and the sanctity of the curriculum were challenged. The commonly accepted beliefs that schools gave everyone a chance to succeed and fairly sorted students on the basis of ability were disputed in court cases, desegregation plans, and critiques of the social-class-based nature of American schools. In the absence of firm cultural support for intellectual demands on students, changes were made. In many schools procedures to safeguard student rights were introduced, graduation requirements fell, the number of electives increased, and homework declined along with teachers' expectations for students. Symbolically, the changes signaled a shift from a cultural priority on academic rigor (now called excellence) and the good of the collective to equity and the rights of the individual. All these changes affected how teachers and principals did their work.

In the mid-1970s a reaction set in. A symbolic manifestation of this reaction was the slogan "back to basics." A bureaucratic one (with its own symbolic implications) was the state testing movement described above. By the early 1980s this reaction was widespread. Although some see the commission reports as the beginning of a reform era, they can also be viewed as a consolidation and symbolic reinforcement of this change. The dramatic language of reports, with their comparisons to the effects of a foreign invasion, references to losing an international competition, and coupling of today's education system to tomorrow's economic health were all ways to galvanize public attention. The kinds of reforms recommended—especially at first—included more school, tougher requirements, more testing, and increased accountability. Whatever their instrumental effects, these changes reflected a shift of priorities back toward academic rigor and the good of the whole, although some argue that the emphasis on equity also declined.

Principals and district administrators found that these reports had symbolic utility. They reinforced values important to principals and teachers. Even before many states passed recommended policies, many districts began making changes in line with the new recommendations. In some districts these changes added even more rigor than the state requirements. This was especially true when high school graduation requirements were raised.

This brief retelling of thirty years of American educational history suggests two lessons. First, the cultural linkages available to principals will depend on themes and changes in the larger society. Sometimes a principal can use these themes; sometimes she must guard against them. Second, a good deal of reform activity is symbolic. Commission reports, presidential meetings with governors, and other events all seem very far away from daily schoolwork. However, they provide material that can be used to reinforce particular themes the principal wants to stress in the school. The principal interested in building a culture for educational improvement should read trends outside the school, downplay those contrary to her intent, and take advantage of symbolic material that can reinforce her initiatives.

CONCLUSION

School culture is not a magic bullet through which the principal can mysteriously redirect the course of education in her school. Instead, it is part of a complex web of linkages that coordinates and guides the actions of teachers. None of these linkages is particularly powerful. Rules and policies can be ignored in the classroom and the effect of culture is limited by teacher isolation. Yet, the full range of linkages is extensive. By building a coherent pattern across them, the principal can have an impact. Such a pattern is difficult to build and maintain. It requires attention to big decisions and day-to-day interactions as well as sensitivity to larger political and cultural trends. On the other hand it may be the most effective way for principals to make a serious contribution to the improvement of the nation's schools.

REFERENCES

Berman, Paul, and McLaughlin, Milbrey. *An Exploratory Study of School District Adaptation*. Santa Monica, Calif.: Rand, 1979.

Bidwell, Charles. "The School as a Formal Organization." In *Handbook of Organizations*, edited by James March, pp. 972–1022. Skokie, Ill.: Rand McNally, 1965.

Deal, Terrence E. "The Symbolism of Effective Schools," *Elementary School Journal* 85 (1985): 601–620.

Deal, Terrence, and Kennedy, Allan. *Corporate Cultures: The Rites and Rituals of Corporate Life*. Reading, Mass.: Addison-Wesley, 1982.

Metz, Mary. *Classrooms and Corridors: The Crisis of Authority in Desegregated Schools*. Berkeley: University of California Press, 1978.

National Commission on Excellence in Education. *A Nation at Risk*. Washington, DC., U.S. Department of Education, 1983.

Peters, Thomas, and Waterman, Robert. *In Search of Excellence: Lessons from America's Best Run Companies*. New York: Harper and Row, 1982.

Wilson, Bruce, and Corcoran, Thomas. *Places Where Children Succeed: A Profile of Outstanding Elementary Schools*. Philadelphia, Penn.: Research for Better Schools, 1987.

Wilson, Bruce, and Corcoran, Thomas. *Successful Secondary Schools: Visions of Excellence in American Public Education*. London: Falmer Press, 1989.

Weick, Karl. "Educational Organizations as Loosely Coupled Systems," *Administrative Science Quarterly* 21 (1976): 1–19.

SUGGESTIONS FOR FURTHER READING

Corbett, Dick, and Wilson, Bruce. *Testing, Reform, and Rebellion*. Norwood, N.J.: Ablex Press, 1991.

Ginsberg, Rick, and Wimpleberg, Robert. "Educational Change by Commission: Attempting 'Trickle Down' Reform," *Educational Evaluation and Policy Analysis* 2, no. 4 (1987): 344–360.

Grant, Gerald. *The World We Created at Hamilton High*. Cambridge, Mass.: Harvard University Press, 1988.

Rossman, Gretchen; Corbett, Dick; and Firestone, William. *Change and Effectiveness in Schools: A Cultural Perspective*. Albany: State University of New York Press, 1988.

Chapter 3

TRANSFORMING SCHOOL CULTURE

Martin L. Maehr and Rachel M. Buck

Newspapers, magazines, and journals have headlined the short-comings of American education. Some claim that American schools are slipping. Others argue that high standards are needed now more than ever before. In either case, there is an urgent need for students who are motivated, competent, and skillful problem solvers. Numerous national studies and reports have addressed these issues and, not surprisingly, a wide array of corporate officials, politicians, and concerned citizens have called for action. Often as not, the call has been for drastic if not radical change. As Thomas Timar (1989) notes, there is hardly an educational system that has not been touched by this call to radically redo teaching and learning. Nationally prominent school districts, including New York City's and Chicago's, have initiated major experiments to revamp schools and learning. Legislators from across the political spectrum have come out in favor of one or another form of restructuring. President Bush also underlined the inclination to move down the reform path in proposing a "crusade to prepare our children and ourselves for the exciting future that looms ahead." The centerpiece of the President's proposal to improve American education is the "reinvention of schooling" in the form of 535 model schools.

School restructuring, of course, is supposed to raise test scores, lower dropout rates, and increase students' competence and their knowledge base. Too often the response to a call for reform represents

The authors are indebted to a number of individuals, especially Dr. Carol Midgley and all members of the Leadership and Learning Research Group.

no real change. A new program is added; the organizational framework is modified. The addition of new programs may simply represent more of the same. Structural change by no means ensures change in process or outcome. In short, the supposed reform, restructuring, or revamping of schools and schooling is often hardly what it pretends to be. The action taken is analogous to rearranging chairs on a sinking Titanic when what we need is a new ship. Teachers often complain about fads in education and with little wonder. Every few years, a new program or technique gains prominence, while a previously proposed remedy for educational problems slips away, perhaps to be recycled at a later date. It is seldom clear, even with seemingly major restructuring efforts, how the action taken will translate into student motivation and learning. What reason or hope, for example, do we have that site-based management will translate into positive student outcomes?

Into this morass of proposal and response we wish to introduce a guiding principle: it is the "culture" of the school that has to change. Clearly, we need to do more than make superficial changes. We need to transform the deepest structures of schooling. More than a new program or two is needed. Improved quality of teacher education by itself is not the answer. Site-based management, teacher empowerment, and changes in leadership styles do not stand alone as solutions. In schools the critical issue is how teachers and students think about, believe in, and value learning—and go about their business of teaching and learning and relating to one another. The success or failure of schools rests on the beliefs and goals that guide the actions of teachers, administrators, and students. To reform schools one must transform school culture. That is the basic argument of this chapter. Indeed, we plan to go beyond that basic point and suggest, further, how school culture can and must be changed.

SCHOOL CULTURE

We sense that each school has a certain "feel," a "character," or a "personality" of its own, and these intuitions are being verified by a growing body of evidence. Early work on educational environments, a plethora of data on "effective schools," and studies specifically on "school culture" have all converged on this central point. Different schools do things differently. They march to different drummers, hold different things sacred, walk and talk in varying manners. They may not seem as exotically different as Minneapolis and Samoa, but they *are* different. Anyone who has experienced schooling in the Mississippi Delta region and on Chicago's North Shore will readily confirm that essential observation. Even schools in the same city often have radically different cultures.

Not only can schools be characterized by a "culture," but the nature of that "culture" determines how, what, and whether children learn. While all schools claim to be about student learning, they in fact stress different purposes and goals and vary in the way they construct their mission. Importantly, they define the nature and meaning of learning in differing ways. But what, more precisely, do we mean by "school culture?"

A Focused Definition

"Culture" is a comprehensive concept, one that has been subjected to a variety of uses. Referring to schools as "having a culture" captures our attention and seems to touch off a set of rich associations related to real-life experiences. Yet, for the concept of culture to be useful to practitioners as well as to researchers, it needs further clarification. What precisely do we mean when we talk about "school culture"?

Perceptions and Goals. We suggest that the concept needs to be narrowed somewhat if it is to be useful. It should embrace significant perceptions, thoughts, and beliefs held by individuals associated with the school. But significant for what? Different answers to that question are possible, but most uses of the term "school culture" imply that it is a *cause of action.* We would suggest very specifically that the bottom line in the study of school culture is the motivation and performance of major participants in the organization. Proposing this as the bottom line narrows our focus considerably. Recent research on motivation has specified the importance of a select group of *perceptions, thoughts, beliefs, and goals* as critical in determining motivation and hence learning. Perceptions that revolve around the purpose of engaging in an endeavor are especially critical. Therefore, we can profitably limit our focus to perceptions of goals and purpose held by individuals who are significant participants in the school context.

Staff and Student Cultures. While such perceptions are important to motivation in all organizations, there is something unique about how the cultures of schools are composed and operate. While there must be a concern with the meaning of workers (teachers and administrators) who produce the "product" (students), it is absolutely critical that special concern center on the meanings as understood by the product. The ultimate bottom line in schools is and has to be the creation of a student who learns—and who acquires a continuing motivation to learn. The culture that engages teachers may not in and of itself lead to desired student outcomes. So there are in effect two interdependent cultures that have to be considered in schools: that of students and that of staff. With regard to students the question is, Does culture influence motivation and learning? With regard to staff the question is, How does the work culture teachers experience translate into creating an environment that fosters student motivation and learning? We focus first on school culture as perceived by students.

SCHOOL CULTURE AND STUDENT LEARNING

All schools purport to have the teaching and learning of all their students as a primary goal. Yet, some define learning in such a way that students are likely to see the whole enterprise as a contest to see who is the best. Other schools give greater place to student growth and worry considerably less about who wins the academic sweepstakes. Still others focus on social goals: "growing up," making friends, conforming to expectations, pleasing parents, getting along. No one school is likely to stress one specific goal to the virtual exclusion of others, but there is increasing evidence that schools differ in the emphases they place on these goals. As such, they define the reasons for being in school.

Goals That Affect Motivation and Learning

What goals are most closely associated with student investment in learning? Fortunately, during the last decade a remarkable amount of research has been conducted on how the individual's beliefs, perceptions, and thoughts about self and the situation affect his or her motivation and learning. Research has found that an individual's *thoughts* about the purpose and goals of engaging in any particular activity are especially important. First, it seems that individuals are most likely to be invested in fulfilling the goals of an organization—virtually any organization—if those goals are clear to them and if they share them. Second, different goals appear to have qualitatively different effects on what individuals do. If the goal is to earn money or to pursue a prize, an individual operates differently than if the goal is to enjoy a reflective moment—or to acquire a skill. Among the possible goals that could be and have been considered, two have emerged as preeminent in expressing the character of the school so far as student motivation and learning are concerned. We will refer to these here as ability goals and task goals.

Ability Goals. Ability goals represent a focus on students' demonstration of ability relative to others. When a student pursues an ability goal, she is likely to be primarily concerned with her performance relative to other students. When teachers and schools stress the demonstration of ability, the standard of success is how well one does relative to others. Not only is social comparison important in defining the nature of success, there is likely to be a competitive edge to the performance, with a few "winning" and the rest "losing."

Task Goals. Task goals represent a concern with the process of learning and the development of skills, knowledge, and understanding. In a word, the focus is on growth. Given this definition of the learning task, it follows that a different meaning system is operative. The standard of success is improvement and its measures are enhanced skills, deepened understanding, and greater knowledge.

Implications for Motivation and Learning. Not surprisingly, these two goals are of critical importance in determining motivation for learning. Given an ability focus, students will characteristically do things designed to make them look smart compared to other students. They are likely to avoid challenging tasks on which they might make mistakes, fail, or appear less intelligent than other children. They are biased toward sure success and not losing their place in the achievement hierarchy.

Task goals, on the other hand, with a stress on growth, tend to minimize the social comparative element, minimize debilitating competition, and orient students toward the intrinsic value of the task itself. With that follows a qualitatively different approach to and an investment in learning tasks. Mistakes are accepted as a natural and potentially productive part of the learning process. They are not a cause for embarrassment, shame, or derision, which often follow when social comparisons are emphasized. Task-focused children are more likely to resist learned helplessness, try harder, and persist longer when faced with a challenging and difficult task. They are less inclined toward taking short cuts to learning, exhibit greater evidence of critical thinking, and, overall, exhibit more productive learning strategies.

In sum, while several goals may describe the nature and character of learning and learning environments, two have emerged as especially important. Carole Ames (in press), John Nicholls (1990), and many other researchers have amassed evidence on how task goals and ability goals represent different meaning systems that lead to demonstrably different approaches to learning. Moreover, as we shall discuss next, it is possible not only to describe the character of a school in terms of stress on these two goals, but also to show how such stresses affect student investment. A particular school's culture is not an inevitability to which teachers and students must resign themselves. A growing body of evidence shows that action can be taken to change the school culture to enhance student motivation and learning.

School Culture Can Be Assessed

If you ask teachers, students, administrators, or parents about school climate and goals, you will find that they readily come forth with clear notions about what the school stresses. Often as not they will also tell you how they feel about these stresses—positively and negatively. They can express these in a standardized form on questionnaires and rating scales that allow for further analyses, portrayal, and replication. This last point is hardly trivial. It is important to the further understanding of the nature and nurture of school culture. It has special significance to those who teach and manage schools. If you can begin to assess school culture—or significant facets of it—in a standardized fashion, then it is possible for any given school to assess its character, evaluate it, and then begin to consider change. In short, the standardized assessment of school culture provides the opportunity for the concept to have wide and practical use.

Goals Are Affected by How Learning Is Managed

Now we get to the heart of our argument: Goals are affected, if not created, by how learning tasks are structured, organized, and managed—and can be changed in ways that will enhance the investment of students. Once having assessed the critical goal stresses, administrators and teachers, parents and community can engage in a self-conscious effort to transform the cultural milieu that is the school. They need not simply react to whatever practices, values, roles, and relationships are extant. The purposes and goals that students adopt for learning are affected by the learning environment. That learning environment, in turn, is affected by leaders and staff action or, in some cases, inaction.

The point is that individual teachers do not alone decide what students do in their classroom. These decisions flow from a shared conception of what schooling is that is embodied in and created by certain policies, practices, and procedures. A classroom's focus on a task goal or an ability goal is significantly determined by which textbooks are chosen, how state mandates are interpreted, how in-service training is planned, and how resources are allocated. Every-day decisions by school leaders, perhaps working with the staff as a whole, their implicit and explicit gestures, their action or inaction, the content of their communication to the central administration and to parents—all these define the range of learning activities that will be made available to students. Several categories of policies, practices, and procedures found in all schools are likely to be important in influencing how students view the purpose of learning. Our goal is to outline several areas for thoughtful consideration and concerted action. Though we give examples, we will not dictate specific actions. Both experience and common sense tell us that what is an appropriate solution in one school and community may be inappropriate in another. Local school administrators and teachers are in the best position to devise new school policies, practices, and procedures. Bear in mind, however, that we are talking about *transforming* school culture, not simply making add-ons or minor changes. Whatever form solutions take, they must foster a task-focused environment by affecting the most basic structures of schooling.

Curriculum and Instructional Practice. A critical element in the school environment is what we expect from students as teaching and learning occurs. Recent research by Phyllis Blumenfeld and Judith Meece (1988) and others shows that the design of the learning tasks affects the perceived purposes and goals of the activity and, consequently, motivation and learning. Students can be given tasks that are relevant to their lives and require creative thinking and problem solving, or they can receive a daily dose of drill-and-practice dittos. In the former case, students are likely to value the task, adopt task-focused goals such as mastering the material, and be intrinsically motivated to do the task. In the case of the latter, students perceive that the purpose of the task is merely to "keep them busy," and students will place little value on the activities involved. They may adopt ability-focused goals such as looking smarter than their peers, which lead to the use of surface-level strategies like finishing their work quickly regardless of the quality.

The definition of any course of study for students is not solely a matter of teacher choice. It is determined by a wide range of factors, but can be influenced heavily by school policy, management, and leadership. Schoolwide resources and attention can be invested in activities that challenge students, stimulate the use of higher-order thinking skills, and engage their intrinsic interest. School policy—*and* school leaders—can stress strict adherence to textbooks or encourage teachers to think broadly and creatively about academic tasks and consider such learning activities as interviews with knowledgeable persons, surveys of constituencies, hands-on and project-oriented activities, project-oriented learning experiences, student-designed activities, and field trips. Teachers can be given (and expected to use) "teacher-proof" texts, worksheets, and preplanned exercises, or they can be given the freedom and encouragement to design and use tasks that are action-oriented, that flow from the interests of the students, and that are challenging and creative.

Student Responsibility and Order. A task goal orientation is rooted in the proposition that doing the task, in and of itself, is the source of motivation. Demanding that someone does a task and using external force or extrinsic rewards to ensure conformance changes the meaning of the task to the person doing it and risks undermining the perception of its intrinsic worth. Thus, it is not surprising that motivation researchers have considered perceived choice as critical in developing a task goal orientation and intrinsic motivation.

Schools, of course, vary in the degree to which students are given a voice in what happens in school, from the courses they take, to the tasks they work on within these courses, to their participation in student governance. In the matter of discipline and order, schools are likely to reflect deeply held beliefs about the purpose of schooling in general and the learning of certain students in particular. In short, maintaining an orderly and safe environment is important, but *how* it is done is equally important as far as establishing the purpose and meaning of learning within a school context. A "safe and orderly" environment for learning can drift into becoming a coercive and stifling environment.

Recognition and Rewards. The use of recognition and rewards is critical in defining what the school stands for and believes in. The varied use of recognition and rewards in school reflects a greater or lesser emphasis on task goals and ability goals. Recognizing the students who get higher grades than other students is a common practice and is flawed in several ways. By design only some students can be recognized, a fact that is hardly motivating to those who have little hope of ever being recognized. The practice defines school and learning as a competitive game in which some win and others lose. With that, it makes winning more important than individual progress in learning and self-development. If, however, the focus is placed on effort put forth and on the progress made in mastering skills and broadening understanding, a different motivational orientation results. In short, recognition and reward practices are important to defining what learning is about and thus to defining the culture of the school as either ability- or task-goal focused.

Grouping. The practice of grouping students together according to their ability level is widespread. Ability grouping within classrooms is common at the elementary level, while assigning students to classes based on their ability is common in middle-level schools, particularly in mathematics. Studies by Jeannie Oakes (1985) show that the resultant groupings send powerful messages to everybody involved in the educational process, particularly students. It encourages teachers, parents, and students to focus on who is "smart" and who is "dumb" and discourages an interest in effort, growth, progress, development. Such concentration on an ability hierarchy serves to create a school culture characterized by an "ability-goals emphasis."

The very pervasiveness and apparent influence of ability grouping practices make it evident that it should be attended to by those who are interested in school culture. Further, this appears to be an area in which those who are charged with setting policy can impact school culture in critical ways. Not that it is easy to make this or any such major change—but grouping practices, like others we have mentioned, are not inevitable.

Evaluation Practices. A large body of literature is available on the effects of evaluation practices on student motivation and learning. Briefly summarized, the findings indicate that these practices are fraught with possibilities for encouraging students to approach academic tasks as competitive contests to see who is the smartest and the best. Focusing as they do on outcome and performance, regardless of the place at which the learner starts, many evaluation practices are likely to suggest that the purpose of teaching is to sort students into categories rather than to assist students in learning. But evaluation practices can also serve to focus students, teachers, and the school staff on a higher purpose: investing in the task for learning's sake. It can reflect a schoolwide belief that all children, their progress in learning, their mastery of skills, and their personal, social, and intellectual growth are the *raison d'être* of the school. Properly employed, portfolio approaches seem to do just that, but so can other evaluation procedures. The overriding point is what kind of definition of school is being presented to children.

Resources. Budgets reflect goals; expenditures reflect values. What an organization believes and wants to do is reflected in the way it uses its resources. The more obvious use of resources involves what can be directly bought: computers, texts, science equipment, library books. In a more subtle and no less important way it also includes intangibles such as in-service activities, retreats, camps, extracurricular activities, school parties, and student government. Schools differ not only in the total amount of resources, but also in the configuration of resources. Even within the bounds of extensive external regulation and policy definition, schools "purchase" different things in different amounts. They also distribute their resources in different ways. These basic observations are obvious to any knowledgeable observer. What may be less obvious is that the array of resources purchased as well as the way they are distributed determine and reflect the culture of the school. For example, many schools have policies that prohibit some students (usually low-achieving students) from gaining access to valued resources, ranging from use of computers to membership in clubs or admittance to school parties. Such policy creates an environment that emphasizes that relative ability is the "coin of the realm." By making participation in some activity contingent on an ability standard, ability goals rather than task goals are stressed.

School staff, especially those in leadership roles, are called on to manage these resources. They do not have unlimited freedom in the resources they obtain and how they distribute them, but they do have choices. We have seen administrators in relatively poor schools somehow manage to find a way to support a teacher who wants to try something new. In schools of similar circumstances we have seen discretionary funds spent not on fostering instructional innovation but to support advanced-placement classes, to send selected students to statewide competitions, and to buy equipment that will be used by a select population in the school. Teachers and students are sensitive to how resources are allocated, particularly since most schools operate on limited budgets, and in this way come to understand what is valued and not valued in the school.

Organization of the School Day. The scheduling of the school day and school activities is an important element in the determination of the learning environment of the school. All of the previously discussed areas interlock and interact with each other in determining school culture as a whole. This is especially true of scheduling. As noted earlier, scheduling influences how students are grouped. It relates to matters of student initiative and responsibility: What choices do students have in controlling use of their time in school? Certain electives may be unavailable to students if the schedule is relatively inflexible. Scheduling dictates how teachers use time and how the curriculum is approached. Team teaching and interdisciplinary approaches to the curriculum are at the mercy of the schedule. Nowhere is this more evident than at the secondary school level, where the school day typically is divided into forty-five-minute periods in which different subjects are taught each period. With this type of schedule, teachers must design tasks that take no more than forty minutes a day. Such time restrictions necessarily limit the types of tasks that students engage in, often resulting in more rote learning tasks and fewer hands-on types of activities. The forty- or fifty-minute period is ill-suited for project-centered instruction. Any teacher wishing to move instruction beyond school walls to a museum or to a garden on the edge of the school grounds will be bound by scheduling policies to a significant degree. The forty- to fifty-minute hour is well designed to reflect a certain definition of teaching and learning that is decidedly didactic and teacher-controlled. More broadly, the organization of the school day reflects, conveys, and influences the culture of the school. And scheduling can be changed. There are choices that can contribute to the character of the school and significantly affect student motivation and learning.

While each of these areas is recognized as an important element in school life, and most are self-evidently a focus for self-conscious decision making and action, few consider how different actions can relate to defining the overall meaning of learning and schooling. Most often, the decisions are seen in isolation from each other; seldom are they seen as proceeding from an overall scheme that affects the culture of the school by transforming task goal and ability goal stresses. Action in each of these areas is critical to determining and transforming the culture of the school and is an important way in which the learning and motivation of students is influenced.

Needed: Task-Focused Schools

At the outset of this chapter we argued that schools and schooling had to change. Specifically, we suggested that a change in culture is needed. It should now be clear that the changes we envision are those that will affect the goals that students adopt in learning. A first and primary objective must be to enhance the stress on task goals and minimize the stress on ability goals. That may ultimately come to mean a wide change in beliefs and practices.

Most schools essentially stress ability goals. That means that "success" in school inevitably means outperforming others on various tasks, especially standardized tests. The recent emphasis on raising educational standards, for example, has focused attention on raising test scores, and many schools have taken to passing out honors to those who obtain the highest scores. Considering the fact that children come to school with different preparation and have different resources available to them in the course of learning, it is inevitable that a great many are doomed to experience failure in school—not just once or twice, but consistently. Should it surprise us that they are likely to lack motivation, become "behavior problems," and ultimately drop out?

Essentially, an ability-focused school never really gives a child a chance to reach his or her potential. He or she is defined, already at the primary level, as (relatively) "smart" or "dumb." The point of emphasizing task goals is to redefine success and thereby change the character of motivation and incentive for learning. Focusing classrooms and the school on task goals is the kind of cultural transformation that is needed. The basis for effective action lies in the examination of the policies and practices we establish or allow.

SCHOOL CULTURE AND STAFF ACTION

We are calling for extensive change and transformation in the way schools define the meaning of schooling. Purposes and goals must be examined and in many cases drastically changed. Business as usual is not likely to eventuate in such efforts. Teachers must rethink how they teach; they must ask questions about the wider environment of learning experienced by students. Simply sticking to one's classroom and to one's subject matter will not do it. The mathematics teacher has to be concerned about schoolwide recognition of students and about what demands for ability grouping might do—not only to his students but to the scheduling of other classes and the character of the school as a whole. More than worry and concern are demanded; more than thinking and discussion are required. Action, experimentation, and a degree of risk taking are needed if cultural transformation is to occur. While the goal is clear, the path of individual schools is not. Thus, we cannot specify precisely what action must be taken. The conditions in a particular school or community will determine this. It is inevitably the case that only those who are embedded in the actions, decisions, and interrelationships know what they are and how to most effectively change them.

Throughout this chapter we have implied that school leadership and staff can have an influence on the school culture experienced by students. The goal of cultural transformation suggests that they can and will use this influence in certain ways. But when and under what conditions will they act to make the changes that affect what students experience, believe, and then do? Transforming school culture involves more than having knowledge about what exists or what can be done. It involves both administrators and staff having the *will* to change. What beliefs are associated with an inclination on the part of leadership and staff to initiate the action that will lead to the kind of school change we envision? That will or motivation to change is likewise a function of certain beliefs, accepted purposes, and goals fostered by the school environment in which the teachers work.

Considerable attention has been given to the work world of teachers in recent years. This research as well as informal observations indicate that this work world changes drastically from school to school. Schools vary in the degree to which they support or inhibit innovation. Teachers may be empowered or excluded from decision making. Resources may be equitably shared, vigorously competed for, or disproportionately reserved for an elite few. Collegiality may pervade or each teacher may go his or her own way. Some schools seem to be bustling with enthusiasm; others essentially demoralized. Continuous staff improvement may be a goal that is clearly seen in schoolwide policy, practices, and procedures—or there is the cultivation of an elite few. Instead of feeling isolated, teachers may perceive open communication, a respect for and valuing of their expertise, an approving recognition of their attempt to improvise and innovate. What among all this variation in the work environments of schools really makes a difference in changing the school along the lines we suggest?

While considerable research has been done that looks at the work world of school staff, little of this work has led to an understanding of what is needed for the kind of transformation we desire. To some considerable degree the study of staff work worlds has gotten little further than determining the convictions that make for a happy, satisfied, and committed staff. While this may be a desirable goal, it is not the ultimate goal we envision. The *sine qua non* by which school reform must be judged is a transformation of the culture of the school that will lead to enhanced student motivation and learning. The extensive literature on job satisfaction stands as a reminder that job satisfaction and commitment, desirable as they may be, do not necessarily yield the kind of outcomes needed. More specifically, the goal is not just that teachers are satisfied, engaged, invested, and committed—it is *how* they go about their task. Are they oriented to providing a motivationally enhancing environment for students? If not, are they open to exploring how this can be done?

What kind of "staff culture" is needed to bring about staff action? We cannot provide the complete answer as yet. But systematic study of this point has been initiated and an outline of possibilities and a few firm results are already available.

Perceptions That Make a Difference

During a school staff meeting to change the culture experienced by students, a second-grade teacher made an interesting and very insightful remark. As she faced the daunting task of changing various school operations to effect change from an ability emphasis to a task emphasis, Ms. T. blurted out: "We need to have the same kind of environment that we're trying to give our students." That remark pointed to an important possibility. Broadly, the teachers' work environment is desirably characterized by goal stresses not unlike those that foster student learning.

It indeed appears that a task goal orientation has positive effects with teachers. A recent study by Moon Ok Lee, Rachel Buck, and Carol Midgley (1992) indicates positive effects when teachers perceive that the school presents them with a work environment that stresses not only the pursuit of excellence but the value of this pursuit for its own reasons. When teachers saw their school as stressing such a task orientation, they were more likely to possess a sense of efficacy, a confidence that they could influence and change their world. These results undergird a point we are making: A certain kind of staff culture is enabling. Specifically, when the work culture stresses progress, improvement, and excellence, it gives teachers confidence not only to take charge but also to take risks, to try something new, to confront a challenge. Social comparison, rigid hierarchies, and competition can be as stifling and debilitating for teachers as for students. The emphasis on improvement and the encouragement to accept mistakes as part of learning and to think of progress in achievement are important for teachers as well as for students.

Creating such an enabling culture for teachers is a big step in the right direction, but it is only a first step. An enabling school culture can be thought of as a harvester of educational ideas and innovations.

But what kind of innovations are being harvested? Do they feed the objective of student learning? Do they increase student motivation, engagement, and problem-solving skills? School leaders need to take the next step and ask not only whether innovations are gathered, but also what kind of innovation is encouraged. School leaders need a way to separate the chaff from the wheat.

Both an increasing core of quantitative data and hands-on experience in a collaborative school transformation project indicate that while staff culture may foster general staff action, it does not necessarily create the kind of action that leads to an enabling task-oriented school culture for students. Work by Rachel Buck, Moon Ok Lee, and Carol Midgley (1992) shows that a staff culture that stresses innovation and excellence does not automatically lead to teachers providing a task-focused environment for their students. In order to create a school culture that leads to students adopting a task goal orientation, school leaders must be specifically and persistently involved with creating, initiating, evaluating, and revising the kind of policies and practices likely associated with a task goal orientation. A school culture that enhances a task goal orientation does not just come naturally when staff is well trained and well treated. Creating a school culture that enhances student adoption of task goals must become the specific and conscious mission of a school.

In order to elicit investment, any organization must make it very clear what it stands for—and some degree of acceptance of and adherence to this "mission" of the organization is absolutely essential. Recently Martin Maehr, Carol Midgley, and Tim Urdan (1992) have suggested the value of a theoretical framework in eliciting integrated staff action toward change. Such theory can provide a shared language of communication and guidelines for effective action. It is the filter through which the value of a given innovation is discerned. When a theoretical framework is effective, programs are not just introduced because someone was inspired by a particular workshop or by a speaker of note. Programs are introduced, shaped, adapted—or rejected—because they fit in with a scheme and serve certain shared purposes and goals. When the reason for action is widely shared within the organization, staff commitment and investment are more easily obtained. An operative, integrative theory that is broadly shared within the organization provides this underlying reason for action. In this sense, theory is critical. Almost every educator has experienced—though not always approved of—the sense of purpose exhibited by those who create "whole language" or some other specialized-mission schools. Some of us can remember the fervor that surrounded "Dewey" or "progressive" or "open" schools. A theoretical framework serves to elicit an important level of commitment, motivation, and action on the part of staff and others concerned with the effective performance of the organization.

Implications for School Leaders. We once asked a principal how he would go about creating a good school. His answer, simply put, was "I just hire good teachers and turn them loose." At first blush this may seem to reflect a desirable degree of modesty or even teacher empowerment. By now, however, we hope the reader finds this a bit troubling.

School administrators must be more than personnel directors. They must provide an enabling work environment for staff where innovation and excellence are the bywords. Beyond this they must take responsibility for engaging staff in the transformation of the school culture experienced by students. Policies, practices, and procedures of the wider school constrain and guide what teachers do in their individual classrooms. Herein lies the opportunity for school transformation. School leaders need to actively engage teachers in the process of school transformation, in examining the result of practices, policies, and procedures on motivation and learning. This can be done most effectively by employing a theoretical framework and a coherent vision that serve as the underlying criteria for all decisions made in the school. The guiding question is, What can be done to create a task-focused learning environment for all students?

Earlier we suggested how school practices for which school leadership is responsible can significantly impact the learning world of the child. Through thoughtful consideration and concerted action educators can change the messages children receive about the goals of learning and as a result affect children's motivation and engagement and the quality of learning they receive. We reinforce that basic point and suggest as emphatically as we can: Leadership can make a difference! Someone has to call the staff to consider the bottom line in which all have a stake. Leaders must not only energize but be persuasive in encouraging a specific direction for change, a course of action that eventuates in cultural transformation that indeed makes a difference in children's learning.

CONCLUSION

We have argued that the nation's schools need a cultural transformation. New programs here and there will not suffice. Restructuring, if merely a matter of toying with governance and power structures, provides little assurance that children's learning will be positively affected. The school culture—the belief system revolving around the meaning and purpose of learning—experienced by students must take on a specific character, a character that is not currently widely evident in schools. We have described the cultural transformation we have in mind and suggested principles and possible strategies to consider in creating it. We offer our argument as a set of hypotheses, but not as an untested argument. Already these ideas have been applied to changing schools, and they are designed to be the subject of continued research, revision, and elaboration, as they are part of a testable theoretical system. As a result, we trust there is a bit of practical wisdom in what we have said as well as a reasonable research agenda for the continuing search for how to make schools places that foster student motivation, engagement, and learning.

REFERENCES

Ames, Carole. "Classrooms: Goals, Structures, and Student Motivation," *Journal of Educational Psychology*, in press.

Blumenfeld, Phyllis C., and Meece, Judith L. "Task Factors, Teacher Behavior, and Students' Use of Learning Strategies in Science," *Elementary School Journal* 88, no. 3 (1988): 235–250.

Buck, Rachel M.; Lee, Moon Ok; and Midgley, Carol. "Teachers' Beliefs, Goals, and Perceptions of the School Culture as Predictors of Instructional Practice." Paper presented at the Annual Meeting of the American Educational Research Association, San Francisco, 1992.

Lee, Moon Ok; Buck, Rachel M.; and Midgley, Carol. "The Organizational Context of Personal Teaching Efficacy." Paper presented at the Annual Meeting of the American Educational Research Association, San Francisco, 1992.

Maehr, Martin L.; Midgley, Carol; and Urdan, Tim. "School Leader as Motivator," *Educational Administration Quarterly* 28 (1992): 410–429.

Nicholls, John G. "What Is Ability and Why Are We Mindful of It? A Developmental Perspective." In *Competence Considered*, edited by Robert J. Sternberg and John Kolligian, Jr. New Haven, Conn.: Yale University Press, 1990.

Oakes, Jeannie. *Keeping Track: How Schools Structure Inequality*. New Haven, Conn.: Yale University Press, 1985.

Timar, Thomas. "The Politics of School Restructuring," *Phi Delta Kappan* 71 (1989): 265–275.

Section II

The Nature of Leadership

Chapter 4

NEW SOURCES OF
LEADERSHIP AUTHORITY

Thomas J. Sergiovanni

The topic of leadership represents one of social science's greatest disappointments. As recently as 1985, for example, Warren Bennis and Burt Nanus (1985) pointed out that despite the thousands of studies of leaders conducted in the last seventy-five years we still do not understand what distinguishes leaders from nonleaders, effective leaders from ineffective leaders, and effective organizations from ineffective organizations. They join a chorus of other social scientists and management theorists who have lost faith in traditional conceptions of leadership.

There are, I believe, two reasons for the failure of leadership. First, we have come to view leadership as behavior rather than action, as something psychological rather than spiritual, as having to do with persons rather than ideas. And second, in trying to understand what drives leadership we have overemphasized bureaucratic, psychological, and technical-rational authority, seriously neglecting professional and moral authority. In the first reason we have separated the hand of leadership from the head and the heart, and in the second reason we have separated the process of leadership from its substance. The result has been a leadership literature that borders on being vacuous and a leadership practice that may not be leadership at all. These are harsh words not spoken lightly.

The bright side of the picture is that in our schools a practice of leadership is emerging that requires us to redefine the concept. The field is ahead of the theory and as a result, we have a literature and an official conversation about leadership that does not account enough for successful leadership practice. To reflect emerging practice we have to move the moral dimension in leadership from the periphery to the center of inquiry, discussion, and practice.

OFFICIAL AND UNOFFICIAL VALUES OF MANAGEMENT

Moving the moral dimension of leadership to the center of practice forces us to rethink some widely accepted assumptions about the values that undergird school management theory. We can group values into three major categories: those that compose the official values of management, those that are not fully recognized (semi-official), and those that are unofficial. The three categories are illustrated in Table 4.1.

Table 4.1

The Values That Undergird School Management Theory

Official Values	*Semi-Official Values*	*Unofficial Values*
Secular authority (I have faith in the authority of the bureaucratic system.)	Sense experience (I have faith in my experiences.)	Sacred authority (I have faith in the authority of the community, in professional norms, in school norms, and in ideals.)
Science (I have faith in empirical findings.)	Intuition (I have faith in my insight.)	Emotions (I have faith in my feelings.)
Deductive logic (I have faith in deductive reasoning.)		

All of the values are legitimate. But in today's practice sacred authority and emotions are neglected and often ignored. When acknowledged, they are often thought to be weak, impressionistic, and feminine concepts. Sense experience and intuition, though acknowledged, do not enjoy equal standing with secular authority, science, and deductive logic. Failure to give equal attention to all of the values leads to impoverished theories of school management and leadership.

How do the values influence practice? Secular authority, science, and deductive logic provide scripts for leaders and others to follow. They rely on technical-rational knowledge that is considered to be more important than the personal knowledge of leaders. Teachers, principals, and superintendents are expected to be subordinate to this knowledge. As a result, discretion is reduced—even eliminated. Without discretion school administrators are not free to decide—they can only do; they are not free to write the script of schools—they can only follow the script that is provided. But without discretion there can be no real leadership.

In recent years sense experience and intuition have made some important inroads in becoming legitimate values of management. The work on reflective practice within the professions is one noteworthy example. This work makes a distinction between scientific knowledge and professional knowledge, claiming that the latter is created in use as professionals solve problems too unique for standard recipes. It suggests that the traditional ways of knowing—secular authority, science, and deductive logic—should inform the decisions that administrators make but should not prescribe their practice. Knowing, it is claimed, is in the action itself as professionals research the context and experiment with different courses of action. Sense experience and intuition have wide currency among practicing school administrators.

Sacred authority and emotion seem also to enjoy wide currency among many school administrators. From the two come such practices as purposing and building a covenant of shared values that bond people together in a common cause and such practice goals as transforming schools from organizations to communities. Hunter Lewis (1990) believes that the operational value systems based on sacred authority and emotion are actually more alike than different. They share, in his view, three features. First, they emphasize the building of group identities and cohesion that make people feel special. Second, they promote a distinct way of life or way of organizing society that provides people with an emotional identity. The third feature, according to Lewis, is that they all require an emotional stimulus such as a mission, a sense of purpose, a covenant of shared values that represents the core or center defining the group as a community. Lewis refers to these value systems as "systems of blood."

Giving more credence to sense experience and intuition and accepting sacred authority and emotion allow for a new kind of leadership—one based on moral authority. Morally based leadership transforms schools from ordinary organizations to communities. This transformation can inspire the kind of commitment, devotion, and service that will make our schools unequaled among society's institutions. But how do we know if this new leadership will work? The answer lies in the extent to which it is able to tap the human will in a fashion that both motivates and inspires.

WHAT MOTIVATES, WHAT INSPIRES?

When I recently asked Catherine Piersall, principal of the San Antonio School in Dade City, Florida, what kinds of events and circumstances in a typical school day made her feel especially good and what kinds made her feel lousy, she responded: "The positive feedback and 'evidence' of successful decisions make me feel especially good. For example, watching a new program, a new approach, a new teacher, and seeing this situation as being successful is very rewarding to me. Another example of something that makes me feel good is to hear good reports on 'my' students who have left our school and are doing well in other school or life situations. The phone call or comment from a parent who tells me that 'Johnny had such problems that year at San An, but thanks to your help he's doing great now.' I feel lousy as a result of the inability to do what I think needs to be done to help a child; the inability to control the situations that lead to inappropriate behavior, learning problems, and the like." It's hard to find any hint of self-interest in her response or that her emotions do not count as she assesses her situation. Nor does Piersall respond as a freestanding individual separate from her commitments to the school and to other groups with which she identifies. Is she an anomaly? Would we have any reason to believe that what matters to her is different from what matters to her teachers or what matters to principals and teachers elsewhere?

From most leadership theory today we would conclude that Catherine Piersall is indeed an anomaly. My research, however, leads me to conclude otherwise. Most current leadership is based on a theory of motivation that has overplayed the importance of self-interest, personal pleasure, and individual choice as the driving forces for what we do. Underplayed are the more altruistic reasons for doing things and the extent to which we identify with and are influenced by membership in groups (such as church, ethnic groups, the teaching profession, school, social networks, neighborhood, nation). The consequence has been a practice that underestimates the complexity of human nature and the capacity of people to be motivated for reasons other than self-interest. We lead with the wrong assumptions in mind. And as a result, the yield in commitment and performance is well under that which most teachers are able to give and want to give to their work. This situation will not improve by trying harder to do the same things, by fine tuning present leadership practices. Improving our yield means changing our outlook.

Traditional leadership theory assumes that we are driven by a desire to maximize self-interest and thus we continually calculate the costs and benefits of our options, choosing those that either make us winners or keep us from losing. Self-interest is so dominant in this thinking that emotions such as love, loyalty, outrage, obligation, duty, goodness, dedication, and desire to help count very little in determining what we do and why we do what we do. Emotions are no more than currency that one uses to get something. Within this view, for example, a loving relationship is considered to be little more than a contract within which two people exchange sentiments and commitments to gain benefits not as easily available outside such a relationship. Work relationships and commitments stem from even more selfish urges.

MORAL JUDGMENT AND MOTIVATION

How realistic is this view of leadership and motivation? One way to find out is by examining your own experiences. When it comes to motivating teachers, students, and parents, for example, do you believe that what gets rewarded gets done? Or, is it your view that when individual self-interest and broader interests are in conflict people are capable of sacrificing the former for the latter? Do you believe that we are capable of responding to duties and obligations that stand above self-interest? Are we, in other words, morally responsive? These questions raise still other questions. When we choose what to do and decide what to be committed to, is the individual the primary decision-making unit and thus free to make independent decisions or do you assume, as does Amitai Etzioni (1988), that groups (ethnic and racial groups, peer groups at work, and neighborhood groups) are the prime decision-making units? In his book *The Moral Dimension*, Etzioni acknowledges that individual decision making exists but that it typically reflects collective attributes and processes, having been made within the context created by one's group memberships.

From Etzioni's research and my extensive conversations with teachers and administrators I conclude that our connections are so important and the process of socialization that takes place as a result of our group memberships is so complete that the notion of individual decision maker is more myth than reality. Further, we humans regularly pass moral judgments over our urges, routinely sacrificing self-interest and pleasure for other reasons. Indeed, a Gallup poll (1988) revealed that 91 percent of the respondents agreed with the statement "Duty comes before pleasure," while only 3 percent disagreed. Our actions and decisions are influenced by what we value and believe as well as by self-interest, and when the two are in conflict values and beliefs often—and for most people typically—take precedence over self-interest. There is, in other words, a bit of the hungry artist in all of us.

WHAT IS IMPORTANT TO TEACHERS?

What does the evidence suggest is important to teachers at work? What motivates them? What inspires them? What keeps them going even when the going gets tough? Is there a fit between the leadership practices of traditional management theory and what is really important to teachers? University of Chicago sociologist Dan Lortie (1975), in his landmark study of teachers in Dade County, Florida, asked his respondents what attracted them to teaching. The themes that dominated their responses were serving others; the importance of working with people, particularly students; the enjoyment they receive from the job itself; material benefits; and the school calendar.

More recently, Harvard University professor Susan Moore Johnson (1990) asked similar questions in her interview study of 115 Massachusetts public, private, and parochial school teachers. Here are examples of the responses from four of the teachers she studied:

- 'The way you could just look into a kid's eyes, the sparkle when you showed them something that they didn't know or that they couldn't understand. . . . There was an energy there that was quite gratifying. It made me want to keep coming back.' [P. 34]
- 'There was something that always attracted me to teaching. I just feel like this is my profession. My bottom line is that I love kids. I get energy from them. I just think they're the brightest people on earth.' [P. 34]
- 'No special reason. I was interested in language. I guess that would be the reason. I started off in Spanish. I thought that teaching would be the best way to make use of what I was studying, because I enjoyed it.' [P. 36]
- 'I feel that God has given all of us a gift to do something. Everybody has a strength. I really believe this strongly, that I can give children education, make them feel good about themselves, let them learn to like to read, let them look at school as Wow! This is wonderful.'[P. 37]

The dominant themes that emerged from Johnson's research were working with students; an interest in the intellectual processes, puzzles, problems; the challenge of pedagogy as an occupation; a commitment to learning more or being more fully engaged in a particular subject matter area or discipline; social purposes in the sense of making a difference in society; religious purposes in the sense of being called to the "ministry" of teaching; and a convenient calender that allowed one to combine career with family or career with other life interests mostly related to personal development. The teachers reported few rewards beyond those gained by working with students and from other aspects of the work itself. They were, for example, dissatisfied with low pay, lack of respect, few opportunities for advancement, lack of administrative support, unnecessary bureaucratic demands, poorly maintained buildings, nonteaching duties, lack of parent involvement, limited autonomy, isolation from other teachers, and the lack of voice in governance and decision making. It appears from Johnson's research that the calling, sense of mission, and commitment to professional, social, or religious ideals are important enough to carry teachers despite the difficulties they encounter in the workplace. Clearly, these teachers are motivated not only by individual self-interest but also by a sense of what is morally good.

It appears to me that the evidence overwhelmingly suggests that self-interest is not powerful enough to account fully for human motivation. We are driven as well by what we believe is right and good, how we feel about things, and by the norms that emerge from our connections with other people. We are driven, to use Etzioni's terms, by morality, emotion, and social bonds. Together the three comprise assumptions underlying a morally based leadership: human beings pass moral judgments over their urges and as a result often sacrifice self-interest for other causes and reasons; people choose largely on the basis of preferences and emotions; and, people are members of social groups and this membership singularly shapes their individual decisions.

SOURCES OF AUTHORITY

Expanding our understanding of what motivates and inspires raises the question of what should be the legitimate bases of authority for the practice of leadership. Bureaucratic, personal, and technical-rational authority pretty much dominate present thinking, and each forces us to think about leadership as something strong, direct, and interpersonal.

Bureaucratic authority relies on hierarchy, rules and regulations, mandates, and clearly communicated role expectations as a way to provide teachers with a script to follow. Teachers, in turn, are expected to comply with this script or face consequences. When this source of authority is prime the following assumptions are presumed:

- Teachers are subordinates in a hierarchically arranged system.
- Supervisors are trustworthy but you cannot trust subordinates very much.
- The goals and interests of teachers and those of supervisors are not the same and thus supervisors must be watchful.
- Hierarchy equals expertise; thus it is presumed that supervisors know more about everything than do teachers.
- External accountability works best.

Most readers will have little difficulty accepting the assertion that bureaucratic leadership is not a good idea. The underlying assumptions are too suspect. Few, for example, believe that teachers as a group are not trustworthy and do not have the same goals and interests as do their supervisors. Even fewer would accept the idea that hierarchy equals expertise. Less contested, perhaps, would be the assumptions that teachers are subordinates in a hierachically arranged system and that external monitoring works best. Leadership theory today, for example, still relies heavily on "expect and inspect," predetermined standards, providing in-service programs for teachers, and providing direct supervision. Because these practices endure, leaders must spend a good deal of time trying to figure out how to motivate teachers and what change strategies to use to get them to do things differently. Leadership, as a result, becomes a direct, intense, and often exhausting activity.

Personal authority is based on the leader's expertise in providing leadership in human relations, in using motivational techniques, and in artfully practicing other interpersonal skills. It is presumed that as a result of this leadership, teachers will want to comply with the leader's wishes. When this source of authority is prime the following assumptions are thought to be true:

• The goals and interests of teachers and supervisors are not the same.
• Teachers have needs and if these needs are met at work, the work gets done as required in exchange.
• Leaders must be expert at reading the needs of teachers and in people-handling skills in order to successfully barter for compliance and for performance increases.
• Congenial relationships and harmonious interpersonal climates make teachers content, easier to work with, and more apt to cooperate.

These assumptions lead to a leadership practice that relies heavily on "expect and reward" and on "what gets rewarded gets done." Emphasis is also given to developing a school climate characterized by a high degree of congeniality among teachers and between teachers and supervisors. The typical reaction of teachers to leadership based on personal authority is to respond as required when rewards are available but not otherwise. Teachers become involved in their work for calculated reasons, and their performance becomes increasingly narrowed.

Suggesting that practicing leadership that relies on psychological principles and personal skills may have negative consequences is likely to raise a few eyebrows. Many school leaders, for example, have worked hard to develop skill in how to motivate teachers, how to apply the correct leadership style, how to boost morale, and how to engineer the right interpersonal climate. These insights are in many ways the "core technology" of leadership. But personal authority cannot tap the full range and depth of human capacity and will and cannot elicit the kind of motivated and spirited response from teachers that will allow schools to work well. Further, overuse of personal authority raises moral as well as practical questions.

What, for example, should be the reasons why teachers should follow their principals? Is it because principals know how to manipulate effectively? Is it because principals can meet the needs of teachers and provide them with other psychological payoffs? Is it because principals are charming and fun to be with? Or is it because principals have something to say that makes sense; have thoughts that point teachers in a direction that captures their imagination; and stand on a set of ideas, values, and conceptions that they believe are good for teachers, for students, and for the school? Emphasizing the former set of questions over the latter provides for a vacuous leadership practice that can lead to what Abraham Zaleznik (1989) refers to as the "managerial mystique," the substitution of process for substance.

Technical-rational authority relies heavily on evidence that is defined by logic and scientific research. Teachers are expected to comply with prescriptions based on this source of authority in light of what is considered to be truth. When technical rationality becomes the prime source of authority the following assumptions are presumed:

● Supervision and teaching are applied sciences.
● Scientific knowledge is privileged and thus superordinate to practice.
● Teachers are skilled technicians.
● Values, preferences, and beliefs do not count very much but facts and objective evidence do.

If proposing that a psychologically based leadership practice is now dysfunctionally being overplayed in schools raises concerns, then suggesting that prime use of technical-rational authority is dysfunctional is also likely to raise concerns. We live, after all, in a technical-rational society where what is considered scientific is prized. But teaching and learning are too complex to be captured so simply. In the real world of teaching none of the assumptions for this view holds up very well, and the related practices portray an unrealistic view of teaching and supervision. There is, for example, a growing consensus that the context for teaching practice is too idiosyncratic, nonlinear, and loosely connected for simplistic conceptions of teaching to work well. As suggested earlier, teachers, like other professionals, cannot be effective by following scripts. Instead they need to *create knowledge in use* as they practice, becoming skilled surfers who ride the wave of the pattern of teaching as it unfolds. This ability requires a higher level of reflection, understanding, and skill than that offered under the guise of technical rationality. Further, the position of professionals needs to be *superordinate* to the knowledge base that supports their practice.

Two additional sources of authority for leadership practice, suggested by an expanded value structure for management theory and by acknowledging the importance of morality, emotions, and social bonds in motivation, are professional and moral. The assumptions underlying the use of professional authority are:

- Situations of practice are idiosyncratic and no one best way to practice exists.
- "Scientific knowledge" and "professional knowledge" are different from professional knowledge created in use as teachers practice.
- The purpose of "scientific knowledge" is to inform, not to prescribe, the practice of teachers and supervisors.
- Professional authority is not external but comes from the context itself and from within the teacher.
- Authority from context comes from the teacher's training and experience.
- Authority from within comes from the teacher's socialization and commitment to the professional ideal.

Leadership based on a professional authority seeks to promote a dialogue among teachers that makes explicit professional values and accepted tenets of practice. These are then translated into standards for professional practice. With standards acknowledged, teachers are then provided with as much discretion as they want and need to hold each other accountable in meeting these standards.

One standard that needs to be developed as we move toward a practice based on professional authority is commitment to the professional ideal. The works of Albert Flores (1988), Alastair McIntyre

(1981), and Nel Noddings (1984) are helpful in developing a conception of the professional ideal suitable for teaching. Professionalism, for example, tends to draw our attention to issues of competence. But competence is not enough. Key to professional autonomy is trust, and trust cannot be earned on the basis of competence alone. Virtue is the other dimension that together with competence defines professionalism. Virtue in teaching is expressed in the form of four fundamental commitments that compose the professional ideal: to practice in an exemplary way; to practice in pursuit of valued social ends; to practice with a concern not only for one's own practice but for the practice itself; and to embody the caring ethnic in one's practice.

Commitment to exemplary practice means practicing at the edge of teaching by staying abreast of new developments, researching one's practice, trying out new approaches, and so on. In a sense it means accepting responsibility for one's own professional development. To pursue valued social ends means placing oneself in service to students and parents and to the school and its purposes. It suggests, for example, that the heart of professionalism in teaching is a commitment to the caring ethic. The caring ethic requires far more than just bringing to bear state-of-the-art technical knowledge to one's practice. Doing only this results in students being treated as clients or cases. The caring ethic means doing everything possible to serve the learning, developmental, and social needs of students as persons.

The concern for the practice of teaching itself is key to the professional ideal. There is, for example, an important difference between being concerned with one's teaching practice and being concerned with the practice of teaching. This latter concern is directed not only to broad issues of teaching knowledge, policy, and practice but to the practical problems and issues teachers face every day in their own classrooms and schools as well. As the professional ideal becomes established in a school it will no longer be acceptable for one person to teach competently without offering help to other teachers who are having difficulty. It will not be enough to have special insights into teaching but not share them with others. It will not be enough to define success in terms of what happens behind one's classroom door when the school itself may be failing.

In *Moral Leadership: Getting to the Heart of School Improvement*, I proposed that professional and moral authority be moved to the center of leadership practices (Sergiovanni, 1992). When professional authority is combined with moral authority the sources of authority for leadership are expanded in important and powerful ways. Moral authority is derived from the felt obligations and duties that teachers feel as a result of their connection to widely shared school community values, ideas, and ideals. When moral authority is in place, teachers respond to shared commitments and felt interdependence by becoming self-managing. The assumptions underlying the use of moral authority are:

- Schools are professional learning communities.
- Communities are defined by their center of shared values, beliefs, and commitments.
- In communities what is considered right and good is as important as what works and what is effective.
- People are motivated as much by emotion and beliefs as by self-interest.
- Collegiality is a form of professional virtue.

As moral authority becomes the prime source for leadership practice the possibility that schools will become transformed from organizations to communities increases. Communities are defined by their center of shared values, beliefs, and commitments. Leaders in communities direct their efforts to identifying and making explicit shared values that then become sources for informal norms that govern behavior. These norms make it possible to promote collegiality as something that is internally felt and that derives from morally driven interdependence. Leaders, as a result, can rely less on external controls and more on the ability of teachers as community members to respond to felt duties and obligations. The school community's informal norm system and the internal connection of teachers to it become substitutes for leadership as teachers become increasingly self-managed.

REINVENTING LEADERSHIP

There is a consensus that leadership is an important ingredient in improving schools. At the same time, few are satisfied with the ways in which leadership has been understood and practiced, and enormous investments are being made to search for better alternatives. In my view much of this effort involves tinkering with a form of leadership that may be beyond salvaging. Leadership itself may be the culprit. No matter how enlightened, when based on bureaucratic, personal, or technical-rational authority its form is direct, external, intense, and control-oriented. As a result, leadership fails to tap fully human potential and to help teachers become self-managing. Expanding the sources of authority for leadership to include professional and moral authority and shifting the emphasis to these two provides some promising alternatives. Since both sources of authority emphasize internal motivation and promote self-management, they can become substitutes for leadership.

REFERENCES

Bennis, Warren, and Nanus, Burt. *Leaders: The Strategies for Taking Charge*. New York: Harper & Row, 1985.

Etzioni, Amitai. *The Moral Dimension: Toward a New Economics*. New York: Free Press, 1988.

Flores, Albert. "What Kind of Person Should a Professional Be?" In *Professional Ideals*, edited by Albert Flores. Belmont, Calif.: Wadsworth, 1988.

Gallup Organization Survey, conducted for the Princeton Religion Research Center, Princeton, N.J., March 11, 1988.

Johnson, Susan Moore. *Teachers at Work: Achieving Success in Our Schools*. New York: Basic Books, 1990.

Lewis, Hunter. *A Question of Values*. New York: Harper & Row, 1990.

Lortie, Dan. *Schoolteacher: A Sociological Study*. Chicago: University of Chicago Press, 1975.

McIntyre, Alastair. *After Virtue*. Notre Dame, Ind.: University of Notre Dame Press, 1981.

Noddings, Nel. *Caring: A Feminine Approach to Ethics and Moral Education*. Berkeley: University of California Press, 1984.

Sergiovanni, Thomas. *Moral Leadership: Getting to the Heart of School Improvement*. San Francisco: Jossey-Bass, 1992.

Zaleznik, Abrahm. *The Managerial Mystique: Restoring Leadership in Business*. New York: Harper & Row, 1989.

Chapter 5

THE VISIONARY PRINCIPAL: SCHOOL LEADERSHIP FOR THE NEXT CENTURY

Marshall Sashkin

More than 50 percent of all current school principals will have retired by the end of the next decade. OERI's (1987) Principal Selection Guide is one step in the direction of improving the increasingly important selection process (which many agree is generally poor, e.g., see Southern Regional Education Board, 1986). But regardless of how they are selected, the next "generation" of principals will be faced with unprecedented opportunities, and with exceptional new challenges as well. Using these opportunities and meeting these challenges will call for a deeper understanding of the role of the principal, along with the skills needed to carry out that role effectively. Principals will need to be "organizational leaders" but even more important, they will have to be *visionary* leaders. I will outline what this means, both in concept and in practice.

Author's Note: An earlier version of this article was prepared as the basis for a presentation to the National Association of Elementary School Principals' Scholars Seminar on July 21, 1987, in Arlington, Virginia. The views expressed in this report are those of the author and do not necessarily represent the positions or policies of the Office of Educational Research and Improvement or the U.S. Department of Education.

THE PRINCIPAL AS AN ORGANIZATIONAL LEADER

Scholars have for some time now recognized that principals have a critical role in school improvement. Ronald Edmonds says it well: "There are some bad schools with good principals, but there are no good schools with bad principals." Recent research confirms that students achieve more in schools whose principals are seen as strong leaders (Andrews and Soder, 1987). But what is "organizational leadership"?

Firestone and Wilson (1985) help by identifying two sets of leadership activities. The first involves creating "bureaucratic linkages," that is, engaging in the managerial and bureaucratic tasks that we normally associate with the role of "administrator." This means creating and enforcing policies, rules, procedures, and authority relations. The second set of activities is less familiar. Firestone and Wilson say that the aim of the activities in this second set is the creation of "cultural linkages." The actions include establishing behavioral norms, using symbols, instituting ceremonies, and even telling stories. All of these actions are designed to build the cultural foundations of organizational excellence.

But let us be more specific, for we can identify several tasks that involve creating these cultural linkages. These tasks have been identified by analyzing the job of the principal on the basis of a wide range of research. Synthesized by Sashkin and Huddle (1988), the list includes the following:

- Establishing an atmosphere conducive to learning
- Setting high expectations for teachers and students
- Setting school-level goals
- Instructional leadership (supervising curriculum and teaching)
- Communicating effectively inside the school
- Building parent and community support

Important as these activities are, they must, for maximum effect, take place in the context of some vision, some broader notion of the nature and meaning of the school. Visions are not, however, generated spontaneously; they are designed and made real by the principal, acting as a visionary leader.

THE PRINCIPAL AS A VISIONARY LEADER

What is this vision? What are its elements, of what does it consist, and to what does it refer? The vision of which I speak is a cultural ideal. It defines the shared values that support certain critical functions of the school organization, functions that must be carried out effectively in any organization if that organization is to survive. These functions have been identified by sociologists and consist of *adapting* to the environment, *achieving goals*, and *coordinating* or integrating the various activities that take place in the organization (Parsons, 1960). There is now some hard evidence that schools in which these functions are accomplished well, by objective assessment, are actually more effective (Hoy and Ferguson, 1985). But what exactly are these shared values? Can they be specified? I think the answer is yes, to a degree. I base this opinion on the recent work on leadership and organizational culture of Edgar Schein (1985), a professor of organizational psychology at the Massachusetts Institute of Technology. Schein discusses the specific content of values in each of the three domains identified above, along with some additional values that are even more basic and general. Recognizing (1) that we are now in the realm of theory rather than fact, (2) that even very different-appearing values can support effectiveness in the same organizational function, and (3) that it is difficult at best to pin down and specify a value, we can use Schein's discussion as the basis for exploring those values that might support the three organizational functions in schools and that might, therefore, be related to school effectiveness. We can then suggest that these are some of the values that should be built into the principal's vision for the school.

Adapting

Schein notes that organizations differ in viewing their environments as controllable, as situations that can be "lived with" in peaceful coexistence, if not outright harmony, or as circumstances to which the organization must concede control. I suggest that the values most likely to support effective adaptation are those emphasizing the organization's control or, perhaps, values centered on the importance of harmonious coexistence. Schein observes that with respect to the question of what value position is best, the answer must depend on which is most accurately oriented to reality. While there is obvious truth to this point, one must also observe that only if there exists the belief that the organization can control its destiny is it likely even to try. Moreover, such trials may well change the "reality," so that the organization *becomes* more capable of controlling its environment and its ultimate destiny. Thus, while it is foolish and perhaps even destructive to hold to values that are in obvious conflict with reality, there is much to be said for taking "optimistic" positions, even when one realizes that there may be some question about whether the value is, in fact, consistent with objective reality. I suggest that to support the adaptation function and to achieve optimal organizational effectiveness, visionary leaders build into their visions the value of control over the organization's destiny and over critical factors in its environment. What are these factors? In most organizations, and in schools, they consist of technology and technological change, of political factors in the larger government bureaucracy as well as at the district level, of the community culture (the school's equivalent of the private-sector organization's marketplace), and of economic conditions. Can schools really control all these things? Certainly not, at least not all the time or completely. Yet the school probably *can* exercise *some* control in each area. New teaching technology can be sought out and implemented. Effective relations must be built at the district level. Finances can be enhanced in a variety of ways. And, building community relations is one of the critical culture-building tasks of the principal. In fact, it should be clear that several of the culture-building tasks are related to this particular value. That should be no surprise; that is what the culture-building tasks are, in essence, all about.

Achieving Goals

Schein suggests that organizational values may emphasize doing and achieving, being, or being-in-becoming, a sort of compromise position. For the school, it would seem that the central values supporting achievement of goals should be doing and achieving, supplemented by being-in-becoming (which is really related to the issue of growth and development, one of the key reasons for the existence of schools). Unlike the case of adapting, there would appear to be little likelihood of a conflict with reality, regardless of which value position is taken.

Internal Coordination

From the work of sociologist James Thompson (1967) it is clear that we think of and treat school organizations as though the many different activities were relatively independent of one another, as though the organization could be coordinated by rather simple methods, such as rules, procedures, and perhaps a few plans. In fact, Thompson's work implies that schools represent extremely complex systems, in which what one teacher or administrator does with regard to a particular student will affect the impact of every other teacher's or administrator's actions with regard to that same student. Under these conditions effective coordination can be achieved only by what Thompson refers to as a process of "mutual adjustment," involving all relevant parties in understanding what each is doing and in working together, explicitly, to make mutual adjustments in their activities in order to achieve their common goals, in this case student learning and development.

Schein (1985) notes that the cultural values relevant to internal coordination center on issues of influence and power. Specifically, the organization may operate under the assumptions that all power and decisions are centrally located and that the system is and should be autocratic. Alternatively, the values involved may be those of democracy and participation, or may reflect "in-between" positions such as paternalism, consultative management, a delegative style, or even a sort of laissez-faire abdication, with everyone pretty much "doing their own thing."

Roland Barth (1987), for example, has characterized collegiality among school faculty as typically analogous to the activity of three-year-olds commonly called "parallel play." However, the sort of coordination needed in schools—what Thompson called coordination by mutual adjustment—calls for a rather high degree of involvement of those who depend on one another, in the process of management and decision making, even requiring consensus at times, with everyone explicitly "buying into" a particular decision or plan of action. It seems, then, that strictly from the pragmatic viewpoint of achieving effective coordination (and thereby contributing to goal achievement), and ignoring the broader sociocultural value of participation in our society, it makes sense to build into school organizations the value of involvement and participation of all faculty and staff in operational decision making.

Schein also observes that organizations take internal coordinative stances emphasizing competition, collaboration, or collateral action on the part of managers and organization members generally. This is relevant to us for several reasons. First, the nature of school organization and its coordinative needs would seem more in line with a collaborative stance. Second, it has become increasingly evident that though schools emphasize competitive values, the real world, for which children are being prepared, is far more oriented toward collaboration, to the reality that most people today work with others to accomplish tasks and attain goals. Richard Walton (1985), of the Harvard Business School, has recently said that the shift to group-based, instead of individual-based, work activity in American organizations represents a revolution in the workplace. If children are to be prepared to live and work effectively in the organizations of the next century, it would seem sensible to build values that support collaborative and collateral activities, along with competition.

I have spent a bit more time on the values underlying effective internal coordination because they are so evidently lacking in American schools. I suggest that visionary school leaders must pay special attention to making these values part of their visions.

Maintaining the Culture

Earlier I referred to certain broader values that provide general support for all three of the critical functions of adapting, achieving goals, and coordinating. At least three such values can be derived from Schein's work. One centers on the assumption that people are "perfectible." Or if we cannot be perfect, at least we can move in that direction. A second value has to do with how we define and determine what is real. Schein describes three ways of defining and determining what is real. The first way is based on physical evidence and the scientific method. The second is based on what others, especially those we trust, respect, and identify with, *say* is real. This is called "social reality." The third test of reality is based on our own personal viewpoints and beliefs, on what we believe to be real for ourselves, regardless of what others may say and even regardless of physical evidence or science. Of course, the latter two tests of reality are much easier to apply when there is a lack of scientific evidence, when there is no empirical proof of whether something is true or not.

There is little support in schools, organizations, or society for the third value, the assumption that what is real is what one personally believes to be (although there is a disturbing trend in the thinking of many identified with "New Age" philosophies toward just such an assumption; e.g., MacLaine, 1983). There is much reinforcement, however, for the second assumption, that what "everyone" agrees is real is what is real. This is especially the case when the issue is complex and when there is little or no scientific evidence in the matter. But it is also worth noting that this value actually supports the values that are the foundations for the three organizational functions, since most of those values, like values in general, are difficult if not impossible to subject to any empirical or scientific test. Now, it should be clear that there is a conflict of sorts here. One value that most educators and most of the public might agree should be emphasized in schools is the value of science as a test of truth, of what is real. To some degree, however, this value might undercut the values that support the critical organizational functions of adapting, achieving goals, and internally coordinating activities.

The conflict here is resolved to a degree by a third general value issue raised by Schein, centering on the distinction between what is *right* and what *works*. This is the difference between moralism and pragmatism. Former Secretary of Education William Bennett has argued that schools are responsible for the development of character in children, for their basic moral education with regard to societally accepted values such as honesty or responsibility. One aspect of the development of moral character is understanding the difference between what is right and what works. Such an understanding reduces or eliminates the sort of conflict referred to above. For example, we should recognize that, as Schein notes, the environment may well exert more control over the school and its activities than does the school over its own "destiny." At the same time, with an understanding of the reality of the situation, we must insist that it is *right*, if not real, that the school exercise some control over its own actions and achievements. With this understanding the visionary principal can act to move the school toward that desired state.

To this point we have analyzed the principal's organizational leadership role—the sets of task activities that principals carry out to create bureaucratic and cultural linkages. We then examined the specific values that effective principals build into their visions of an ideal school culture, one that supports the critical organizational functions of adapting, achieving, and coordinating. We must finally ask what actions principals take to make real their visions of a cultural ideal.

VISIONARY LEADERSHIP IN ACTION

There are three major aspects to visionary leadership in action. The first consists of constructing the vision, creating this ideal image of the school and its culture. The second involves developing an organizational philosophy that succinctly states the vision, along with the programs and policies to put the philosophy into practice. The third aspect centers on the leaders' own practices, the specific actions in which leaders engage in order to create and support their visions on a one-to-one basis.

Visioning: Creating a Cultural Ideal

The process of conceiving a vision calls for certain cognitive skills. Central to this is the ability to think in terms of a period of time, that is, not just in terms of daily or weekly goals, but in terms of actions carried out over a period of years. Elliott Jaques (1979) has shown that there are reliable differences among individuals in terms of the span of time over which they think and work. Effective executive leaders must, according to Jaques, be able to think clearly, to "vision," over periods of at least five years. In more recent work Jaques (1986) has constructed a theory of cognitive development, based on Piagetian concepts, specifying in detail the series of hierarchical cognitive tasks required to construct visions over increasingly long spans of time. The details of Jaques's theory are far too complex to review in a brief manner; about all I can say here is that school leaders should be able to create visions that can be realized over a three- to five-year time span.

Implementing the Vision Organizationally

Elsewhere I have outlined the process by which visionary leaders turn their cultural ideals into organizational realities (Sashkin, 1985, 1988). The key to this process is creating an explicit organizational philosophy and then enacting that philosophy by means of specific policies and programs. The specific statement of the philosophy is best developed by the leader and his or her key subordinates. In this manner, the visionary leader begins the process of implementing the vision with a strong base of support from the key actors in the system. The statement of philosophy must then be put into practice, by means of actual, operational policies and programs. That is, the philosophy must be articulated through action, not just words. Terrence Deal (1987) provides some details as to how this process of articulating the vision takes place. He speaks of identifying heroes, of creating rituals and ceremonies, and of telling stories that support and strengthen the philosophy and the values that underlie the philosophy, and that make more visible the policies and programs derived from the philosophy. Deal also notes that this process is best accomplished if the visionary leader can identify an "informal network of cultural players," of teachers who are informal advisers (or even just gossips), of secretaries or custodians who, in effect, preside over the school's culture, serve as key links to the community, and are keepers of the school's history. These are the keys to organizational implementation of the leader's vision.

Implementing the Vision Through Personal Practices

Finally, effective visionary leaders put their visions into practice by means of their own specific interpersonal behaviors on a one-to-one basis. There are at least five important sets of such behaviors, which I have detailed elsewhere (Sashkin, 1986, 1988). In brief summary, visionary leaders enact their visions through effective communication practices (such as active listening, the effective use of feedback, and asking questions well). A second set of actions centers on expressing the vision (or important elements of the vision) in unusual, exciting, and attention-grabbing ways. Third, visionary leaders are consistent in their actions: They do not "waffle," lie, or change positions easily; they are seen as reliable and worthy of a high degree of trust. The fourth set of actions has to do with exhibiting and expressing respect for oneself and for others, making one's own self-confidence clear to others, and making others feel valued, especially with respect to their roles in carrying out the leader's vision. Finally, visionary leaders act to create risks that organization members can buy into and share, both in action and outcome. These are not unrealistic or long-shot risks but are sensible, with high but not unattainable goals. There is

o act in the ways just described are

harismatic" (Sashkin and Fulmer,

ctor in the visionary leader's ability

ganization to carry out the leader's

LUSION

ie that effective schools must have

ders are those who can create and

s culture that contains within it the

t. As organizational leaders, princi-

tors (although effective administra-

ant); they must be culture-builders

principal understands the critical

e—adapting, achieving, and co-

that support these functions. But

more than understanding is needed. Effective school leaders must be able to conceive of a vision, a cultural ideal, for the school. They must be able to generate schoolwide support for this vision, by involving others in articulating a philosophy that summarizes the vision and by creating policies and programs that turn the philosophy (and the vision) into action. Finally, effective school leaders carry out their visions through their own specific behavioral practices, as shown by their interpersonal behavior. None of this is easy, conceptually or behaviorally. Yet it is only through the actions of visionary principals that we can attain the ideal of effective schools.

REFERENCES

Andrews, Richard L., and Soder, Roger. "Principal Leadership and Student Achievement," *Educational Leadership* 44, no. 6 (1987): 9–11.

Barth, R. "Personal Vision and School Improvement." Address before the annual convocation of the Academy for the Advancement of Teaching and Management, Princeton, N. J., 1987.

Deal, Terrence E. "The Culture of Schools." In *Leadership: Examining the Elusive*, 1987 Yearbook of the Association for Supervision and Curriculum Development, edited by Linda T. Sheive and Marian B. Schoenheit, pp. 3–15. Alexandria, Va:

Association for Supervision and Curriculum Development, 1987. (Also, reprinted as Chapter 1 in this volume.)

Firestone, William A., and Wilson, Bruce L. "Using Bureaucratic and Cultural Linkages to Improve Instruction," *Educational Administration Quarterly* 21, no. 2 (1985): 7–30.

Hoy, Wayne K., and Ferguson, Judith, "A Theoretical Framework and Exploration of Organizational Effectiveness of Schools," *Educational Administration Quarterly* 21, no. 2 (1985): 117–134.

Jaques, Elliott. "Taking Time Seriously in Evaluating Jobs," *Harvard Business Review* 57, no. 5 (1979): 124–132.

Jaques, Elliott. "The Development of Intellectual Capability: A Discussion of Stratified Systems Theory," *Journal of Applied Behavioral Science* 22 (1986): 361–383.

MacLaine, Shirley. *Out on a Limb*. New York: Bantam, 1983.

Office of Educational Research and Improvement. *Principal Selection Guide*. Washington, D. C.: U.S. Government Printing Office, 1987.

Parsons, Talcott. *Structure and Process in Modern Societies*. New York: Free Press, 1960.

Sashkin, Marshall. "Creating Organizational Excellence: Developing a Top Management Mind Set and Implementing a Strategy." Paper presented at the annual meeting of the Academy of Management, Organizational Development Division, San Diego, 1985.

Sashkin, Marshall. "True Vision in Leadership," *Training and Development Journal* 40, no. 5 (1986): 58–61.

Sashkin, Marshall. "The Visionary Leader: A New Theory of Organizational Leadership." In *Charismatic Leadership in Management*, edited by J. A. Conger and R. N. Kanungo. San Francisco: Jossey-Bass, 1988.

Sashkin, Marshall, and Fulmer, R. M. "Toward an Organizational Leadership Theory." In *Emerging Leadership Vistas*, edited by J. G. Hunt et al. Boston: Lexington Press, 1987.

Sashkin, Marshall, and Huddle, G. "A Synthesis of Job Analysis Research on the Job of the School Principal." Unpublished report. Washington, D. C.: Office of Educational Research and Improvement, U. S. Department of Education, 1988.

Sashkin, Marshall, and Huddle, G. "Recruit Top Principals: Tips for Spotting and Coaching Key Players," *School Administrator* 45, no. 2 (1988): 8–13, 15.

Schein, Edgar H. *Organizational Culture and Leadership*. San Francisco: Jossey-Bass, 1985.

Southern Regional Education Board. *Effective School Principals*. Atlanta, Ga.: Southern Regional Education Board, 1986.

Thompson, James D. *Organizations in Action*. New York: McGraw-Hill, 1967.

Walton, Richard E. "From Control to Commitment in the Workplace," *Harvard Business Review* 63, no. 2 (1985): 77–94.

SECTION III

Leadership and Culture

Chapter 6

STRATEGIES FOR BUILDING SCHOOL CULTURES: PRINCIPALS AS SYMBOLIC LEADERS

Terrence E. Deal and Kent D. Peterson

Policymakers and parents are demanding quality schools. The key question troubling most practitioners is, How do we create the kind of schools that we can all be proud of? Quality comes from a particular combination of top-flight instruction, carefully designed curriculum, and effective school leadership. But behind any quality organization—school or otherwise—is the inner, unspoken set of values and purposes that weave quality into the daily routine and motivate everyone to do his or her best. This inner reality is often overlooked by educational leaders, but it is a key part of quality schooling and it influences the regular ways that people do things and shapes the underlying norms, values, and beliefs of schools. This inner reality is called the school's culture. In this chapter we discuss the ways that principals can and often do shape this underlying set of purposes, beliefs, and folkways to create high-quality educational experiences.

For decades, principals have used terms like "climate" or "ethos" to understand and capture illusive but powerful patterns and forces in their schools. Borrowing a term from anthropology, we have labeled these ethereal influences "school culture." Culture describes the character of a school and reflects deeper themes and patterns of core values, common beliefs, and regular traditions that develop over time. This culture often exists outside conscious awareness and underneath everyday life, but it shapes everything inside the school. This culture "consists of the stable, underlying social meanings that shape beliefs and behavior over time" (Deal and Peterson, 1990, p. 7).

The importance and influence of school ethos or culture is demonstrated in both research and practice. The culture of an organization can influence productivity, the commitment to improve, professional development, and the underlying ways that teachers and administrators organize and coordinate complex activities in highly diverse settings, including classrooms (Bolman and Deal, 1992). For example, schools that share strong values related to student achievement can increase the attention, time, and resources that are applied to helping students learn. This occurs not because of explicit rules and procedures but because the importance of student achievement is woven into the underlying purposes and patterns of all of the rules, actions, and procedures.

School cultures valuing improvement support risk taking and change not through formal procedures or structures but through unstated norms and shared understandings about what is valued and important. In schools where educators share values and beliefs about education and teaching, coordination occurs implicitly through shared beliefs and unstated ways of acting. It does not occur through job descriptions, contractual obligations, or administrative oversight. While leadership must focus on the technical quality of curriculum and instruction, leaders must also focus on shaping the underlying culture of the school (Sashkin, 1987). Effective leadership must be both administrative and cultural in its scope (Kouzes and Posner, 1990; Schein, 1985; Wilson and Firestone, 1987).

Cultural leadership incorporates, supports, and transforms the norms and values of those who have been part of the school long before the principal arrived and will probably be there long after the principal leaves. The principal shapes the underlying culture of the school through a variety of means. Shaping the culture of a school is not like remodeling a house. The principal must take into consideration several key issues. The process begins with understanding or "reading" the existing culture and then progressively moving to actions or behaviors that mold or reinforce desirable core values and norms.

First, the principal must be alert to the schools' inner character: its history, traditions, values, beliefs, and folkways. Second, the principal, as cultural leader, examines what exists in the school and compares it to notions of what a quality school is. Where the existing culture matches the nature of a quality school, the principal seeks to *reinforce* existing patterns. Where the existing culture does not support quality schooling, the principal attempts to change it over time. Through daily brief activities, as well as long-term planning, the principal works with others to *reshape* and *remold* the culture of the school. Principals cannot manipulate or reshape a culture through sheer force. A culture must be transformed through incremental steps that reinforce new values and new beliefs about quality and excellence.

To read or understand the underlying culture of the school, the principal and other leaders need to look below the surface of what is really happening and closely watch how people act and the values they espouse. What are the symbols, rituals, and traditions that support what is really going on? What may seem to be unimportant or mundane events may carry great symbolic weight. For example, in one school the opportunity for teachers to go off as a team for five days to brainstorm, plan, and discuss school improvement strategies was an important tradition that reinforced existing norms of quality and collegiality.

In addition, leaders can reconstruct a school's history by listening to the stories of past events or examining artifacts and records such as faculty meeting agenda, newsletter stories, and school goals. Prior efforts at school improvement, crises previously faced by staff, or the leadership style of the previous principal all contribute to the current state of affairs. Re-creating a school's history helps the principal to understand where the school came from and how the culture developed. Once the culture is understood, the principal may consider trying to shape it.

School cultures are shaped through a variety of means. Principals, particularly because of their formal positions and visibility, assume five key roles in shaping social tapestry. Principals act as (1) *symbol*, (2) *potter*, (3) *poet*, (4) *actor*, and (5) *healer*.

As symbols, principals reinforce and mold school values through their dress, daily behavior, and attention to or appreciation of events and routine activities. They communicate beliefs about teaching and learning by what they read, talk about, or call attention to.

In the role of potter, principals consciously and unconsciously shape school culture by identifying school heroes and heroines (exemplars of core values). The principal also convenes daily rituals and develops traditions and ceremonies. These symbolic activities connect people to core values, by communicating and reinforcing dramatically what the school stands for.

As poets, principals shape culture through the use of language. The principal paints images of improvement, weaving words or metaphors and spinning tales to focus the culture. How much principals and others talk about students, discuss techniques for improving instruction, or prompt deeper analysis of student needs shapes the school's beliefs and assumptions. Principals live in a verbal environment; a good 70 to 80 percent of their day is spent in oral communication. What they say, the words they use, and even the tone of their delivery send messages and ideas that reinforce core purposes and values.

Another important role is that of principal as actor. Here, the principal is a key member of an ensemble capable of shifting situations or scripts with ease, portraying or dramatizing a consistent set of values and a clear, direct vision. In addition, the principal must be able to improvise in the inevitable dramas, crises, and comedies that make up a school's daily life. As an actor, the principal takes on many roles during important events. These roles provide opportunities to reinforce and mold underlying norms and values.

Finally, the principal is a healer, overseeing and ministering to transitions and changes in the life of the school that naturally produce a sense of loss or hurt. The principal marks beginnings and ends with ceremonies and works with individuals and groups to cope with any rift or tear in the school's social fabric.

The principal shapes school culture in daily routines and yearly rhythms. The roles of symbol, potter, poet, actor, and healer often combine and merge during crises and major transitions, but they also exist independently to shape the meaning and purposes of the school.

Principals shape organizational cultures in a variety of ways. In a series of case studies Deal and Peterson (1990) illustrated six major ways that school principals shaped the culture both formally and informally:

1. Developing a sense of what the school should and could be.
2. Recruiting and selecting staff whose values fit with the school's.

3. Resolving conflicts, disputes, and problems directly as a way of shaping values.
4. Communicating values and beliefs in daily routines and behaviors.
5. Identifying and articulating stories that communicate shared values.
6. Nurturing the traditions, ceremonies, rituals, and symbols that communicate and reinforce the school culture.

These six strategies of building culture were exhibited in the daily work of five principals.

The five cases originate from a variety of sources: (1) original research on Henry Cotton, Principal of Cherry Creek High School in Cherry Creek, Colorado (Peterson, n.d.); (2) Frances Hedges, an inner-city school principal studied by the Far West Regional Laboratory (Dwyer, 1986); (3) Ray Murdock, a rural school principal also studied by the Far West Regional Laboratory (Dwyer et al., 1984); (4) Robert Mastruzzi, a New York high school principal detailed in Lightfoot (1983), *The Good High School*; and (5) Frank Boyden, headmaster of Deerfield Academy portrayed by John McPhee (1966) in *The Headmaster*. These cases provide excellent, concrete material for illustrating the ways that principals shape culture.

DEVELOPING A SENSE OF WHAT IS IMPORTANT

Each of the five principals had a clear notion of what her or his school stood for. Henry Cotton focused primarily on academic performance and quality. Frances Hedges, the inner-city school principal, valued academic performance and focused on improving reading skills and students' self-esteem. Robert Mastruzzi, the New York secondary school principal, emphasized diversity, attendance at school, and helping less fortunate members of the school as a way to communicate that the school is promoting support and inclusion of all people. Ray Murdock, the rural school principal, concentrated his attention on the importance of students' academic growth and on making the school feel like a "family." He sought to ensure that his school was a model of rural education with a caring school climate for every child—no matter how difficult his or her home situation. Frank Boyden, the private school headmaster, regularly emphasized that he, the staff, and the school were there only for the students. He valued loyalty and commitment to the school and to its students.

While these principals had similar concerns for quality and for serving their students, each identified a particular value-based vision for the organization. What is key is not that the vision had a particular set of values but that the values were clear and well articulated. These principals and the headmaster had "a clear and focused sense of mission or values" (Deal and Peterson, 1990, p. 81). And, they stuck to these purposes over time.

SELECTING FACULTY

A second important approach was to carefully recruit and select faculty based on their "fit" with the school. Selecting the staff was not just a technical activity, the process went deeper and focused not only on the candidates' skills and abilities but also on their values.

Each principal approached the task differently. Henry Cotton worked hard to recruit faculty who shared the values he was trying to inculcate. He also helped existing faculty who did not fit in to find positions in other schools. Frances Hedges was considerably restricted in her right to hire and recruit teachers, because of strict transfer policies and few open positions. But she drew on her knowledge and districtwide contacts to attract teachers who shared her values. In three years Hedges had built a substantial core of like-minded faculty. Because his school was new, Mastruzzi was able to screen and hire a brand-new faculty. He looked for teachers who not only could perform well with inner-city students but shared the school's emerging values. Murdock in his rural setting had the opportunity, over sixteen years, to hire almost every teacher at his school. He interviewed prospective staff members carefully to ensure that their values were consistent with those of the school as a whole. Finally, Boyden selected faculty who were loyal to Deerfield Academy and its students. He made sure the teachers were committed to the work of the school as defined by the core values of Deerfield. It took these principals different lengths of time to get faculty who could share, express, and articulate the core values of the school, but their common quest for quality faculty helped shape the culture of their schools.

DEALING WITH CONFLICT

Each of these principals was clear about what was important. They defended their values in the midst of conflict and pressure. They used conflict to communicate educational values and to reinforce widely held beliefs about teaching and desirable social norms.

While none of these principals (and headmaster) was hesitant about dealing with conflict, each confronted conflict in different ways. Cotton was direct and, at times, highly confrontational in his dealings with students and teachers, especially those whose activities or behaviors conflicted with the core purpose of the school. Hedges tried to build a sense of collaboration among her faculty because of prior divisiveness. She used a conflict with a reading teacher as an opportunity to convene a faculty retreat to resolve the issue collectively. Mastruzzi's style was also more collaborative than confrontational, but he did not shy away from conflict or pressure. He dealt fairly with community and teachers but was not afraid to face conflicts over core issues that came up. Murdock seemed to have few major current conflicts to cope with. In the past he had faced resistance in seeking resources and in gaining parent support. This took considerable energy and time. He did not hesitate to deal with present problems and worked to solve them. Boyden, unlike the other public school leaders, had considerable power and personal influence over faculty members and others. As a group, these leaders found ways of dealing with conflict and problems to communicate core values. They shared a willingness to deal directly with difficulties that would otherwise undermine a sense of collective purpose.

SETTING A CONSISTENT EXAMPLE

These five leaders consistently communicated their values through their behaviors and actions. Cotton was seldom without a book from which he quoted liberally. In doing so he showed concern for self-development and academics. Hedges's convictions were constantly identifiable in her everyday behavior. While at school she picked up litter, praised outstanding students, and worked extremely hard. Mastruzzi communicated his beliefs by regularly listening to others, showing interest in school activities, and touring the building. By paying attention to people, to activities, and to the physical character of the school, he exemplified school. Murdock created formal ceremonies and traditions to nurture schoolwide values. He set an example of service by supporting the school, helping individuals, repairing equipment himself, and even serving food in the cafeteria. Frank Boyden provided a different set of examples. Even as he passed normal retirement age, he rose early every morning and worked late into the evening. His behaviors communicated the kind of commitment and dedication he expected. Every moment of his life was focused on the school, its faculty, and its students. He pulled weeds on the lawn, picked up pieces of litter, and gave pep talks to athletes. He strove to make the school spotless and energetic.

In different ways all five school leaders communicated values through daily routines and concrete actions as a way of reinforcing the culture.

TELLING STORIES THAT COMMUNICATE VALUE

Telling stories about the school's history and the successes of teachers and students provides another medium for communicating values. Cotton relied on a voluminous treasure house of stories that communicated hard work, collaboration, and success. Mastruzzi frequently told stories of academic and athletic success. Boyden told and retold the story of the Deerfield hero who had been a student, an athlete, a faculty member, and later a war hero. Though we do not have evidence of Hedges and Murdock as storytellers, one can imagine the stories they might tell. Stories about school heroes and heroines, shared experiences, and hard work communicate aspects of principals' values and vision.

CEREMONIES, TRADITIONS, RITUALS, AND SYMBOLS AS CULTURE BUILDERS

Ceremonies, traditions, rituals, and symbols are some of the most commonly recognized ways of building culture. These special events communicate values, beliefs, or hopes for a school. While graduation ceremonies clearly and explicitly communicate values, daily routines do as well. Cotton elevated ceremonies into a formal and traditional part of school life. Hedges regularly integrated symbolic routines such as schoolwide assemblies and poetry readings in her school. Mastruzzi developed a tradition of collecting Christmas gifts for the needy to highlight the school's values of helping the less fortunate. Murdock conscientiously created complex celebratory ceremonies and traditions to provide a cornerstone for his school culture. He held an annual art auction, a yearly carnival, special days, and scheduled meetings with each child on his or her birthday. This helped build the close community he was seeking.

Boyden established important small rituals to communicate values. For example, he distributed grades personally to each student, and his day-to-day routines of touring and talking often seemed to have a deeper purpose. They communicated his valuing of quality.

Each school leader, some more and some less, used formal cultural elements to define, shape, and express the culture he or she was seeking to reinforce. It is clear that these principals understood the value of ceremonies and rituals as media to communicate values.

FURTHER EXAMPLES

Principals everywhere communicate values and shape their cultures in these six ways. Many principals communicate a sense of what is important. In one school a principal who was closing two schools had a "funeral" ceremony. The event marked the closing of one school and the incorporation of its students into the new school. With high ceremony members of the school community carried the artifacts of the old school to the new school, thereby reinforcing the value of continuity and history. In another school, named after the famous environmentalist John Muir, principals and staff spent a week celebrating John Muir's life and used his example as a way to communicate the values that they shared.

Principals undoubtedly try to select faculty with strong teaching skills, but many principals also seek faculty whose values support the core purposes of the school. In one midwestern school a principal spent all summer identifying and selecting (holding over thirty interviews) teachers that he needed, but also teachers who may qualify in the future for his academically successful, culturally diverse school. Another principal both interviewed new faculty and socialized them into the school's values of collaboration, collegiality, and improvement.

Principals shape their culture by facing conflicts as a way to communicate the values they hold. One midwestern high school principal went to the city council to have a request from a local gas station/grocery store for a permit to sell beer turned down because it was located half a block from the school. In raising the issue she communicated her commitment to blocking easy access to drugs nearby, thereby reinforcing the school's drug-free values.

Principals also regularly communicate values through their actions and routines. One western high school principal spends two minutes every day in every classroom. In another school the principal regularly sends out articles and research on new instructional ideas even though it may be years before they will be used. A third principal attends summer training programs, thus communicating his professional commitment to being an instructional leader.

More and more, principals are rediscovering the art of storytelling. Telling stories is a key element of culture building and one of its enjoyable sides. But not all stories are positive. A southern principal had to remold a school's culture. The school's prevailing story was about "thirty-four graduates of the high school who were in prison." To overcome this negative story, which was typically shared with all incoming students and teachers, the principal invited thirty-four graduates who were successful in all lines of work to an alumni ceremony. The "thirty-four graduates story" is now focused on these successful alumni. It communicates a different cultural meaning of success and membership.

More principals are also identifying ceremonies, traditions, rituals, and symbols to communicate their values. Increasingly, principals are using the granting of tenure as a time to reconnect teachers to the values of serving all children. In other schools, beginning-of-the-year ceremonies are used to communicate values. One West Virginia district, for example, brings everyone together at the beginning of the school year to share in the successes of the prior year and to celebrate the hopes for the new year.

SUMMARY AND CONCLUSIONS

How do we ensure quality schools for all students? How do schools develop communities where teachers and principals engage in self-sustaining, continuous renewal, and improvement? These ends require more than changing rules and procedures; they require a

strong school culture that sustains and nurtures collegiality, performance, and risk taking. Key to establishing and sustaining these positive school cultures is a principal who can read the existing culture
and who has the will and the ability to reinforce and reshape the
culture to support quality and equity. Though we have emphasized
the leadership role of the principal, symbolic leadership can also come
from teachers, parents, and others.

To help all students succeed, schools must have strong ties to
constituents, effective systems of teaching and learning, and a set of
norms, values, and beliefs that nurture and sustain continuous
growth. These features are often embedded in the culture and routines
of the school.

REFERENCES

Bolman, Lee G., and Deal, Terrence E. *Reframing Organizations*. San Francisco:
  Jossey-Bass, 1992.

Deal, Terrence E., and Peterson, Kent D. *The Principal's Role in Shaping School Culture*.
  Washington, D. C.: U. S. Department of Education, Office of Educational
  Research and Improvement, 1990.

Dwyer, David C. "Frances Hedges: A Case Study of Instructional Leadership,"
  Peabody Journal of Education 63, no. 1 (1986): 19–86.

Dwyer, D. C.; Lee, G. V.; Barnett, B. G.; Filby, N. N.; and Rowan, B. *Ray Murdock
  and Jefferson Elementary School: Instructional Leadership in a Rural Setting*. San Francisco: Instructional Management Program, Far West Laboratory for Educational
  Research and Development, November 1984.

Kouzes, James M., and Posner, Barry Z. *The Leadership Challenge*. San Francisco:
  Jossey-Bass, 1990.

Lightfoot, Sara L. *The Good High School*. New York: Basic Books, 1983.

McPhee, John. *The Headmaster*. New York: Farrar, Straus and Giroux, 1966.

Peterson, Kent D. Unpublished study of Cherry Creek High School. Madison, Wisc.,
  n.d.

Sashkin, Marshall. "A Theory of Organizational Leadership: Vision, Culture, and
  Charisma." Paper presented at a symposium on Charismatic Leadership in
  Management, McGill University, Montreal, 1987.

Schein, Edgar N. *Organizational Culture and Leadership*. San Francisco: Jossey-Bass,
  1985.

Wilson, Bruce, and Firestone, William. "The Principal and Instruction: Combining
  Bureaucratic and Cultural Linkages," *Educational Leadership* 45, no. 1 (1987):
  18–24.

Chapter 7

PRINCIPALS AND THEIR SCHOOL CULTURES: UNDERSTANDINGS FROM QUANTITATIVE AND QUALITATIVE RESEARCH

Marshall Sashkin and Molly Goltman Sashkin

Only in the past decade have researchers begun to study leadership in schools, in contrast to "administration." It was not so long ago that Stogdill (1973) wrote that the only type of leadership in schools was laissez-faire leadership. This was largely a consequence of training educational administrators to be "good bureaucrats" and nothing more. But that image of school leadership has been changing and will change still more.

That effective schools have effective leaders has become an axiom of the "effective schools" literature (e.g., see Edmonds, 1979; Purkey and Smith, 1983). Bossert (1985), for example, observed that studies of effective elementary schools consistently show that such schools have in common "a school principal who is a strong programmatic leader" (p. 39).

Much has been written recently about the leadership role of

An earlier version of this paper was presented at the Annual Meeting of the American Educational Research Association, Boston, 1990. The views expressed here are those of the authors writing in their private capacity and do not necessarily reflect the positions or policies of the Office of Educational Research and Improvement or the U. S. Department of Education.

school principals (see, for example, Sheive and Schoenheit, 1987; Sashkin, 1988a; Sergiovanni, 1987). Indeed, there has been progress toward selecting effective school leaders (U. S. Department of Education, 1987) based on the most current concepts of leadership as "transformation" (e.g., see Burns, 1978; Schein, 1985). A recent Illinois law suggests that practitioners and state policymakers have started to engage this issue. This law requires all school principals to spend at least 51 percent of their time as "instructional leaders."

It has become more and more common to read and hear that the essential factor underlying effective schools is an "ethos" or "culture" of excellence, and that effective school leaders are *culture builders*. This idea began in the more general treatment of "corporate cultures" developed by Deal and Kennedy (1982) and applied by Deal (1987) to the school context. Deal speaks, for example, of telling stories about heroes, establishing ceremonies, and engaging in culture-building rituals. These are all examples of actions used by effective school leaders to create cultures of excellence.

Despite progress in understanding school leadership, relatively little attention has been given to the development of quantitative measures of school leadership. Only recently has some work begun, including that to be described here. But our purpose is not to replace a qualitative focus on school leadership with one based on quantitative research. Instead, our aim is to show how evidence gathered through each of these research traditions can be seen as complementary and can provide a more complete (and complex) understanding of how school leaders build culture.

The work presented here represents some initial efforts to measure and understand school leadership and school culture, and to examine the relationship between them. The first part of this chapter reports quantitative data obtained in a study of a single, entire (but relatively small) school district located near a major city. The study itself was in part a vehicle for collecting data using new questionnaire instruments designed to assess school and district culture. The quantitative evidence presented provides, we believe, sound support for the conclusion that leadership and culture are causally intertwined.

The second part of the chapter explores the way school leaders build cultures, using qualitative methods to explore and understand such work. The arguments presented derive in part from the current work of Deal and Peterson (1990) on the culture-building role of the school principal and in part from Sashkin's research on school leadership (Sashkin, 1987, 1988a; Sashkin and Burke, 1990).

QUANTITATIVE MEASURES OF LEADERSHIP AND CULTURE BUILDING

The Marshall County School District is a small but growing district located about twenty miles from a large urban area. It is becoming increasingly a "bedroom suburb." The area is strongly middle and upper-middle class and its twelve schools generally share a good reputation for educational quality (though some, of course, are more highly regarded than others). In this study of leadership and culture building, the *Leader Behavior Questionnaire* (Sashkin, 1988b; Sashkin and Burke, 1990) was used to obtain data from (and about) all administrators in the district, including at the building level the principals, assistant principals, lead teachers, and vocational supervisors, and in the central office the superintendent, associate superintendent, and assistant superintendents. Questionnaires to assess school culture were distributed at random to five teachers in each school and to twenty professional personnel in the central office.

The Measures

The *Leader Behavior Questionnaire* (LBQ) has ten scales. Three subscores and a total "Visionary Leadership" (VL) score can be derived from scores on the ten scales. The first five scales assess specific leader behaviors identified by Bennis (1984) and by Bennis and Nanus (1985) as characteristic of exceptionally effective leaders. We have named these scales "clarity of communication," "communication skills," "consistency" (trust), "caring" (respect for self and for others), and "creating opportunities." Scores on these five scales are added to give a subscore on "Visionary Leader Behavior" (VLB).

The next three scales assess certain characteristics thought to be associated with transformational (or visionary) leadership. The first (scale six) measures self-confidence, the belief that one can have an effect on one's environment (Bandura, 1977). The second (scale seven) assesses one's need for power directed in socially positive ways (McClelland and Burnham, 1976). The third (scale eight) measures time span of vision, a surrogate for a form of cognitive complexity identified by Jaques (1986) and basic to his theory of organizations and leadership. By summing the scores on these three scales a sub-score on "Visionary Leadership Characteristics" (VLC) is obtained.

The third and final section of the LBQ contains two scales de-signed to assess the extent to which the leader has been effective in building the organization's culture. One (scale nine) is based on Parsons's four functions of adaptation, goal attainment, integration, and pattern maintenance (Parsons, 1960; Sashkin, 1987). The other (scale ten) assesses the degree to which the leader has been able to incorporate into the organization's culture certain values thought to facilitate effective functioning (Schein, 1985; Sashkin, 1988a). By adding scores on these two culture-building scales a third subscore on "Visionary Culture Building" (VCB) is obtained.

A total Visionary Leaderhip score (VL) is obtained by summing the scores on all ten scales of the LBQ.

The second questionnaire used, part of one distributed to teachers in each school, was the "School Culture Assessment Questionnaire" (SCAQ). It was designed to assess the effectiveness with which the organization performs the Parsonian functions. These functions are labeled "cultural strength" (latent pattern maintenance), "managing change" (adaptation), "teamwork" (integration), and "achieving" and "community orientation" (goal attainment). The goal attainment function is split into two scales because external (client/customer) goal focus is so often ignored by organizations (Peters and Waterman, 1982) even though it is a potent source of problems (Perrow, 1970).

The other part of the second quantitative measure was a question-naire developed by Sashkin and Morris (1987), based on work by Bolman and Deal (1984) that analyzes human behavior in organiza-tions by using four different perspectives: structural, political, human resource, and symbolic. The questionnaire assesses the extent to which people in an organization think in terms of one or another of these perspectives, or "frames of reference," and is referred to as the "Frames of Reference" (FOR) questionnaire.

Method

An average building leadership score was calculated, using all LBQ scores obtained from administrators in each building (and in the central office). This yielded an overall school (and an overall central office) leadership score. Independently, three to five persons in each school (and sixteen individuals in the central office) responded to the culture questionnaires. Within each school (and for the central office) the scores were averaged to obtain building (or central office) scores for school culture. Note, then, that we used the number twelve to calculate the statistical significance of the results, for the twelve schools. Our "n" (twelve) is *not* the total number of respondents, which is much larger. The analysis correlates LBQ scores (recall that these are not individual scores but represent building or district-level leadership scores) with culture assessment scores (also at the building or district level).

Both the leadership and the culture measures are, thus, based on aggregated individual responses. There is stronger reason to feel comfortable with this procedure with regard to the culture measures than with respect to the measure of building leadership. That is, the leadership questionnaire is an assessment of the action of a specific individual. We are making the assumption that we can legitimately aggregate the specific behaviors of all the administrators in a building, although there is some reason to be wary of such an assumption. However, the School Culture Assessment (SCAQ) and the Frames of Reference (FOR) questionnaires were specifically designed to gather organization-level perceptual data. Thus, there should be no reason to question the legitimacy of aggregating individual responses on the two culture assessment questionnaires.

This study suffers from few responses per building for the measures of school culture. We believe, however, that this weakness is more than offset by the fact that unlike most correlation studies the data come from completely independent sources so that there is no possibility of bias arising from same-source data.

As used in the present study, both the LBQ and the culture assessment questionnaires must be seen as experimental instruments. The LBQ has considerable research support, suggesting that it is a valid measure of leadership (Sashkin and Burke, 1990). However, the way it is used here, as an aggregated assessment of building-level leadership, must be considered experimental. The SCAQ and the FOR are both still under development; neither is a well-tested instrument.

A final weakness in the present study is a product of the small sample size—twelve schools. This places severe limits on the size of the effects that must be present to detect significant results. Because of the small sample size, correlations must be quite high, about .60 or more, to be statistically significant at the .05 level.

RESULTS

Despite the stringent limit on statistical significance, many of the intercorrelations were significant and many were substantial. Note that our prime interest is in the relationship between leadership and school culture, but a secondary interest is whether there are any consistent relationships between the two culture measures.

Visionary Leadership Behavior and Culture

Recall that the first five scales of the LBQ assess specific behavioral dimensions identified by Bennis in his study of ninety exceptional leaders. Communication skills showed a strong and significant relation to the culture-function measure "teamwork" ($r = .69$). The same was true with respect to the "creating opportunities" scale and teamwork ($r = .58$). The caring scale showed consistent positive relationships with most of the culture-function measures (on the order of $r = .40$) but, especially, with overall culture strength ($r = .72$). Caring (respect) also showed a moderate (nonsignificant) negative relationship to the structural frame of reference and a similar but positive relationship to the symbolic frame of reference. Finally, consistency (trust) showed strong relationships with most of the culture measures, including achievement ($r = .48$), change ($r = .57$), teamwork ($r = .73$), community orientation ($r = .51$), structural frame of reference ($r = .56$), political frame of reference ($r = -.43$), and human resource frame of reference ($r = .69$). What this suggests is that trust, developed by consistency of action, is a potent culture-building force. This single behavioral factor may help to instill values of achievement, effective adaptation, teamwork, and a positive community orientation, while encouraging organizational operations that are consistent with effective administrative structures and a sound human resource orientation. And, at the same time, this trust factor seems to discourage a power/political frame of reference.

In sum, the visionary leader behavior scales are clearly and significantly associated with more effective team functioning, and the total VLB score has a significant positive relationship to teamwork. These results support our thesis that leadership behavior and culture are related and, more specifically, that the more one engages in these visionary leadership behaviors, the better the organization's culture looks in terms of Parsons's crucial four functions (adapting to change, achieving goals, working as a team, having a strong shared set of values and beliefs, and having a strong focus on the external community). If there is any surprise here it is with respect to the strong and consistent relations found between trust behaviors and just about all the culture measures. Also of interest is the similar (but somewhat less strong) pattern of correlations found for caring behaviors and the culture measures. Perhaps this is because these leader behaviors, trust and caring, have especially strong effects on people's feelings. This would logically, then, relate to individuals' experiences of the organization's culture.

Visionary Leadership Characteristics and Culture

For two of these three scales, self-confidence (scale six) and empowerment (scale seven), we find no exceptional relations with the culture measures. Self-confidence shows a moderate relationship to cultural strength but it is not significant. Neither scale has any substantial relations with any of the four cultural frames of reference defined by Bolman and Deal (1984). However, when we look at our measure of the third personal characteristic (scale eight), long-term vision (a simplistic surrogate for Jaques's [1986] cognitive complexity/time span of discretion variable), we find some highly significant relationships. Time span (long-term vision) relates strongly to change orientation ($r = .56$) and has modest positive relationships with all of the other cultural functions. Time span is also negatively related to the political framework ($r = -.61$) and positively related to leaders' use of the symbolic framework ($r = .70$). This suggests that the political framework carries negative connotations. The relationship between time span and the use of symbols supports Jaques's concept of time span/cognitive complexity as an underlying and crucial factor in visionary leadership. The notion of culture building as involving the use of symbols (expressed by Deal and Peterson in Chapter 6 in this book) is also supported. The overall

Visionary Leader Characteristics (VLC) score is positively (but not significantly) related to cultural strength and to the symbolic framework.

Overall, these results highlight the importance of a long-range sense of vision as a factor in successful culture building. Leaders with such vision are more likely to be found in schools with cultures scored high on Parsons's dimensions.

Visionary Culture Building and Culture

The remaining scales were developed to assess, first, the extent to which a leader is able to have a positive impact on the four Parsonian functions (scale nine, organizational leadership) and, second, the degree to which the leader is able to instill within the organization's culture the specific values that support the effective operation of those functions (scale ten, cultural leadership). The organizational leadership scale showed moderate (but significant) relationships with change orientation (adaptation) and with teamwork. The cultural leadership scale relates significantly to cultural strength (r = .52) and moderately to change orientation and to the symbolic framework, but not to any of the other culture measures. The summed Visionary Culture Building (VCB) score is significantly related both to strength (r = .50) and to change (r = .55), but only modestly to teamwork and the symbolic framework, and not at all to the remaining culture measures.

Overall, there was a pattern of clear and strong relationships between the visionary culture building measures and the independent assessments of school culture.

Visionary Leadership and Culture

The overall Visionary Leadership (VL) score—simply the sum of the ten scales—relates positively to all five cultural function scales. The relationship is, however, significant for teamwork (r = .58) and (significant but weak for) achievement orientation (r = .46). There is a small positive relation to the symbolic framework (r = .36) but not to any other of the frameworks.

To look briefly across the ten scales, the three summary scales, and the total Visionary Leadership score, we find consistent positive relationships with the independent culture measures. These relationships generally conform to what one would expect based on one or another of the current theories of visionary or transformational organizational leadership (e.g., see Bass, 1985; Bennis and Nanus, 1985; Burns, 1978; Sashkin, 1988b; Sashkin and Burke, 1990). The present results provide solid support for our notions of what it is that leaders who build effective cultures do, how they behave, and what sort of characteristics they possess.

QUANTITATIVE MEASURES: SOME CONCLUSIONS

Our primary conclusion is that leadership and culture, independently measured, are indeed interrelated. Overall, what we have been calling visionary leadership behavior (Sashkin and Burke, 1990) relates most strongly to effective integration—that is, teamwork. Perhaps more important, trust and respect seem especially significant for producing cultures in which the critical functions operate effectively. Sashkin and Williams (1990) have recently shown that the climate of fairness (based in part on trust and respect) that managers create by their actions relates significantly to bottom-line costs (measured as costs of employee sickness and of accident compensation).

Turning to the characteristics of effective leaders, the strong—and sensible—relations between time span of vision and (1) cultural change orientation (adaptability), (2) the use of a symbolic framework for understanding the organization, and (3) the avoidance of a political framework are all intriguing. Culture building, as defined and measured here, does seem related to cultural strength and effective adaptation, and that is encouraging. Finally, the overall visionary leadership score does indeed relate to effective cultural functioning and perhaps to the use of a symbolic framework as well. These results are all consistent with visionary leadership theory as initially defined by Sashkin and Fulmer (1987) and extended by Sashkin and Burke (1990).

The study reported here is a step in the development of a quantitative understanding of school leadership. We have seen that we can accurately measure certain characteristics that are associated with the ability to act effectively as culture-building visionary leaders, specific behaviors that such leaders use to construct cultures, and some of the organizational-level outcomes of their efforts. These are theoretically and practically important results, but they are not enough.

Our quantitative measures yield an understanding of the "why" of effective school leadership. They illustrate the relationships between leadership and cultures that are effective in promoting organizational and individual excellence. Yet we do not mean to imply that a qualitative understanding of how school leaders build culture is unimportant. In fact, such qualitative knowledge is crucial. While we have focused on quantitative measures of culture and leadership behavior directed toward culture building, we are convinced that the key to building effective school cultures will be found in two areas: in the way school leaders *think* about culture building (in terms of strategies) and in *how* these school leaders use the specific behaviors we have measured to construct school cultures. If we are ever to connect the academic research on school leadership, we must do so by examining the "how" of leadership, in a qualitative manner.

To explore this we turn to the recent work of Deal and Peterson (1990), which we will extend by using our own notions of leadership. We will show how school principals construct effective cultures through both strategic leadership approaches and concrete leadership behaviors.

EXAMINING THE QUALITATIVE ASPECT OF SCHOOL LEADERSHIP

Deal and Peterson (1990) have recently produced an analysis of case studies of effective culture building by principals. In their report they draw on the work of Schein (1985) and others to provide a framework for understanding culture building. They focus on five specific action strategies school leaders use to build effective cultures. Our report builds on these five themes, most of which were pursued in one way or another by each of the five exceptional principals whose actions were subjected to in-depth case analysis. Our argument, however, differs in three important ways from that of Deal and Peterson. First, we made certain assumptions about how the five strategies fit together, with some taking a primary and others a secondary and somewhat different role. Second, our argument differs in its explication of the underlying problems and challenges in applying the five strategies. Finally, the present approach attempts to place the principal's culture-building role in a broader context of school leadership.

The five themes identified and described in detail by Deal and

Peterson (1990) involve (1) staffing, (2) conflict, (3) modeling, (4) telling stories, and (5) creating traditions, ceremonies, and rituals. We will look at how each strategy is composed of two types or "levels" of tactical action. At the first such level we see relatively obvious activities. At the second and more subtle level we find some new insights on the use of each strategy and the difficulties involved.

Strategy 1: Value-Based Staffing

The headmaster of an old, successful private school was asked what his first actions were when he stepped into the role five years earlier. He said, "Well, I guess I picked as my key staff people who shared my own philosophy, who had beliefs about education similar to mine." Selecting (or removing) staff based on the congruence or fit (or lack of such) between their educational values and those of the principal is a critical strategy for effective school leadership and culture building. In each of the five cases reviewed by Deal and Peterson (1990), the principal or headmaster had identified and selected (or, in some cases, removed) staff based on his or her under-lying values and beliefs. This was the case even when the principal lacked formal authority to hire or fire.

One principal (Dwyer et al., 1984a) who had no such power was nonetheless able eventually to select compatible staff by letting "the right people"—individuals she had come to know well during her twenty years in the district—know about forthcoming openings. Of course, it was a more difficult process without formal staffing author-ity, and it took some time—three years—to build a cadre of deeply committed staff who shared and supported the principal's vision and values. Still, this effective principal was able to accomplish this due in part to her long-term vision (Sashkin, 1988a).

There must be a core group of like-minded individuals who can identify with and support the principal's values. Only then can the principal successfully instill those values within the school's culture, thereby building a foundation for excellence. At least some members of that core group will probably have to be selected into the school. Selecting key staff may sound difficult because principals typically lack the authority to do so, but this is not the sole or even the most significant challenge. Rather, the real difficulty is in (a) knowing how to identify the underlying educational values and beliefs of potential staff members and (b) having the skill to apply that knowledge.

To sum up, there are two aspects to value-based staffing:

1. On the first, relatively obvious and perhaps superficial level— *ways must be found to select staff members who share the principal's values (or to remove those who hold opposing values).*
2. On the second, deeper and more subtle level—*skills are needed and must be used to identify individuals' values and to decide whether those values will strengthen or weaken the desired culture.*

Strategy 2: Using Conflict Constructively

It is well known that facing and dealing with, or "confronting," conflict is generally the best and often the only way to resolve conflict constructively (Thomas, 1976; Sashkin, 1989). Yet how often does one hear about principals who "hide" from disputes in their offices, or who use written rules and rigid procedures as "fair" ways to deal with differences and disagreements? But withdrawal is never a solution. And while rule- or third-party-based compromises and bargains may not be unfair, neither are such approaches seen as fair by the parties involved. Fairness is in the eye of the beholder and results only if that "beholder" is a satisfied party in the resolution (Maier, 1963).

One of the cases reviewed by Deal and Peterson (1990), that of Frances Hedges (Dwyer et al., 1984a), shows clearly the effective use of conflict as a culture-building strategy. Hedges confronted faculty who disapproved of her installation of a reading specialist to assist them in various ways (reading was a key priority at the school and Hedges considered improving reading skills a basic and unquestioned value). Her approach was to call a weekend retreat to work on the issues and problems and to develop resolutions that involved the reading specialist as well as teachers.

An obvious prerequisite for dealing constructively with conflict is to confront it, rather than ignore or avoid it. But a less recognized factor concerns the development and use of shared values to resolve conflicts. Common values can anchor whatever resolution the conflicting parties come up with, both ensuring the success of the solution and strengthening the shared culture. Without a framework of superordinate values, it is not likely that the parties can deal with the conflict in a "win-win" or problem-solving manner. At best, the parties might arrive at a reasonable compromise or a fair bargain. Bargaining and compromise, though not necessarily destructive, are almost never constructive. Dealing with conflict constructively means developing a creative, integrative resolution that meets the desires of all the parties (Sashkin, 1989).

For example, Frances Hedges made sure that the retreat did not simply open up professional turf wars between teachers and the reading specialist. Instead, she focused their attention on how to support the overarching value of strong reading skills. Thus, the strategy of using conflict constructively to build culture calls for the active involvement of all parties. But even more important is the use of the conflict-resolution process to tie the issues back to—and to reinforce—shared beliefs and values.

There are, then, two important tactical aspects to managing conflict constructively.

1. On a somewhat superficial level—*conflict must be openly examined and dealt with, never denied or avoided.*
2. On a deeper level—*resolution of conflict must begin by explicitly identifying shared values, which can then serve as the basis for a solution.*

Strategy 3: Modeling Values in Action

By their behavior, effective school leaders actively model the values on which they strive to build school cultures. In one sense, this is simply conformance with the commonplace but true aphorism, "Actions speak louder than words." Words can clarify, explain and interpret, draw attention to, and reinforce values and thus help to build and strengthen cultures. But directly observable action— preferably involving interaction with others—is more effective than speech for instilling values that guide subsequent actions.

Where this becomes more challenging is not just in the doing but in the design and the doing over time. That is, to effectively model and strengthen cultural values, one's behavior must be persistent, consistent, and, in a sense, planned. Only repeated action ensures that others will clearly see the values one models as guiding that action. And, only when actions are consistent in illustrating the same or complementary values will those values be seen as an operative (and not just an espoused) aspect of the school's culture (Argyris and Schön, 1974).

These two requirements are unlikely to be met by chance, without some degree of forethought about one's aims (although that forethought may not involve formal planning and may be based more on instinct and intuition than on any sort of identifiable program). This is one reason people say that effective leaders have vision. Such leaders think in terms of the future, not just for the moment. D. Quinn Mills, a management scholar at the Harvard Business School, has said, "Leaders live in the future, and planning is their language."

Deal and Peterson (1990) review the case of Ray Murdock, principal of an elementary school in a poor, rural area of a southwestern state (this case was initially developed by Dwyer et al., 1984b). Murdock's overriding value during the sixteen years he had been principal was to create an environment in which children felt personally cared for. This value of caring was, for Murdock, primary and pervaded his actions. For example, he met with each student on that child's birthday to talk about achievements and plans. When Murdock had "cafeteria duty" he would serve food to children in the line, and as they passed he would make personal contact with each one. These are but two specific examples of a large set of behavioral actions that served to model the value of personal care.

There are two aspects to the modeling of values:

1. At the first, superficial level—*the specific actions of the principal count more than the words the principal uses to espouse values.*
2. On the second, deeper level—*values must be "designed" into actions, with constancy and consistency.*

Strategy 4: Telling Stories About Heroes and Heroines

We often think of storytelling as relating fairy tales to children—and this is a very powerful way of acculturating children to the norms and values of a society. But telling stories can also illustrate a school's culture to adults. Thus, it is important to remove and discard the implicit "for kids only" label often attached to storytelling.

As do leaders in other types of organizations (Deal and Kennedy, 1982), successful school leaders typically use stories that illustrate the values embodied in the school's culture. Telling stories both reinforces those values and strengthens the culture. While this is not universal, it seems that most leaders identify archetypes and create metaphors. They then use these metaphors and archetypes to define and clarify values through inspiring stories that illustrate the effective operation of those values.

In *The Headmaster*, John McPhee (1966) writes about Frank Boyden, headmaster of a private school during the first part of this century. Perhaps the most central value Boyden saw as critical to the culture he was building was that of commitment to the school and its students. Boyden often told of a faculty member whose commitment to the students was so great that he rejected an offer from another school that would have increased both his prestige and his income. "He's not in it for the money," Boyden would say.

It is important to note that the stories used are not simply made up or manufactured to illustrate a point. Stories used to define and reinforce basic beliefs and values *must* be true. Of course, the storytelling principal will interpret the "raw facts," making sense of the story in terms of certain values and beliefs, but this is different from inventing a tale.

Some principals probably avoid storytelling simply because they do not see themselves as good storytellers, or do not feel they have the required communication skills. This is a real but superficial reason. That is, the effective use of stories in this way requires not merely an interesting story and not just good storytelling skills. It also requires a deep appreciation of the importance of stories as vehicles for defining and reinforcing values. The more complex skills needed by principals as storytellers include identifying archetypes and metaphors that, in an inspiring way, define and illustrate the successful operation of the values the principal promotes. This can be a difficult conceptual task, calling for skill in thinking of and using symbols.

Thus, we have two aspects of using stories to clarify and reinforce cultural values:

1. At the first, more superficial level—*involves applying sound interpersonal communication (storytelling) skills.*
2. At a more difficult and far deeper level—*stories must be constructed so that they clearly connect to specific values, applying archetypes and metaphors to a concrete example.*

Strategy 5: Creating Traditions, Ceremonies, and Rituals

These are formal and semiformal patterns of behavior, some typically large-scale (ceremonies) and some usually small-scale (rituals), that recognize and "celebrate" the values that define the school's culture. Traditions and ceremonies accomplish this in highly visible, formalized ways, while rituals usually do so through somewhat less grand but much more frequent patterns of action.

Frances Hedges, of whom we spoke earlier, did not use ceremonies, but relied on many behavioral modeling routines that themselves became almost ritualized. For example, she made sure she was highly visible as she visited classes and monitored the hallways. Often she would just happen to "bump into" teachers who had grown accustomed to expect her to ask about exceptional student work at this time. This way Hedges gave teachers an opportunity to tell her about one or another outstanding student paper or achievement. Through this ritual Hedges showed her concern for the value of increasing the self-esteem of children (indicated through the report of recognition and reward of the student by the teacher). Furthermore, not only did the student look good but the teacher also gained recognition. Also reinforced was the value Hedges placed on reading and language skills. It was clear the ritualized situation that Hedges created led to enhanced positive feelings for all those involved.

There is an obvious problem with ceremonies, traditions, and rituals: they take time to establish and to carry out. Time is no insignificant issue for most principals whose days are typically fragmented and filled with buzzing, booming confusion. But time is not the most important problem. The real difficulty is in building into the event the values to be illustrated and reinforced. This must be done in ways that create strong positive affect, thus leading those involved to internalize the values. Constructing inspiring traditions, rituals, and ceremonies is difficult. Ray Murdock, mentioned earlier, was exceptionally creative in doing so. For example, he started the tradition of an annual student art auction, at which students' drawings were sold to the highest bidder. Murdock ritually purchased the first item himself. In this way he demonstrated by his action the deeply held value of caring for students.

There are two aspects of creating traditions, ceremonies, and rituals:

1. The more superficial aspect of this strategy—*use of traditions, ceremonies, and rituals requires good time management, planning (implicit and explicit), and the effective use of scarce personal and organizational time.*

2. The more subtle and deeper level—*involves creating traditions, ceremonies, and rituals that connect clearly to cultural values and involve participants in a positive emotional manner (and that may also uproot and replace negative traditions and dysfunctional beliefs)*.

Primary and Secondary Strategies

The first three strategies define and construct culture by embedding values in the day-to-day actions of people in the school. The latter two strategies *clarify* and *reinforce* those values, but do not usually by themselves construct culture or instill values. Principals build values into the school's culture—or, perhaps more properly, school cultures are constructed of values—only through value-based behavioral actions. These actions must involve the actual "business" of the school: teaching, learning, and administering teaching and learning. This is not to suggest that storytelling and traditions are of little consequence; they can be powerful tools for expanding peoples' understanding of values and for reinforcing the values on which the culture is built. There is, however, a far more important primary and secondary distinction to be made, in terms of tactics used to implement the five strategies.

Primary and Secondary Tactics in Using the Strategies

For each of the five strategies described above we identified two levels of difficulty in the effective use of that strategy, that is, in the "tactical" application of the strategy to the task of culture building. At one level the difficulty was fairly obvious and, while perhaps not easy or simple to deal with, was unlikely to be a crucial problem. Thus, a principal who has inadequate communication skills for effective storytelling might see this as "the" problem in using stories to reinforce culture. But such communication skills can be developed by almost anyone, certainly by someone with the ability to attain the position of school principal. The real problem, the more subtle and generally unrecognized issue, is that of constructing a story that really gets at a particular value, and does so in a way that is both concrete and metaphorical. Doing that is much harder than just telling a story. Constructing a story that interprets the school's history in a way that reinforces certain cultural values is a difficult tactic for school leaders to apply.

Similarly, finding time for major ceremonies or minor rituals is an obvious—but not the crucial—problem in using traditions, ceremonies, and rituals. Effective time management is a useful tactic in applying the strategy of using ceremonies and rituals to strengthen culture. However, a deeper, more subtle, and far more important tactic involves the value-linked design of such activities. For each strategy we found one relatively superficial factor: taking actions that illustrate values, in the case of the modeling strategy; recognizing and confronting conflicts to deal with them, in the case of conflict management; and finding ways to get like-minded key staff, in the case of value-based staffing. And in each case we identified a much more important, deeper, and more subtle tactical issue: designing one's actions as part of a coherent value-based culture-building strategy; using conflicts to identify and internalize common superordinate values among the parties involved; and developing the skills and methods needed to identify the values of potential staff members and determine whether those values will support or undermine the culture the principal is building. This line of thought—contrasting the two aspects of each strategy, the superficial and the deep—leads to a deeper understanding of the nature of leadership.

Levels of Leadership

The work of Firestone and Wilson (1985) makes it strikingly clear that school leadership has two essential categories of activity. One set is called building bureaucratic linkages. This means doing the required administrative "chores" that keep things going smoothly: filing reports, scheduling meetings, making sure students get on the busses on time (and that the busses are there for them to board), and so on. Firestone and Wilson go on to describe a very different but no less important category of activity that they call building cultural linkages. What they refer to, of course, is very much what we have been talking about: the creation of strong cultures built on values that link action to excellent outcomes.

It has become common to think of the first set of activities as management and the second as leadership. Two of the foremost management and leadership scholars of our time, Peter Drucker and Warren Bennis, have observed, "Managers do things right; leaders do the right things." But it is not quite that simple.

As part of their program of research at the National Center for Research on School Leadership (at the University of Illinois–Champaign/Urbana) Martin Maehr and his associates arranged for a group of about fifty principals in the greater Chicago area to participate in what he calls "the beeper study." Each principal agreed to carry a paging device, the kind that makes a "beep" when one receives an urgent telephone message; physicians often wear these devices when they are on call. The beepers were programmed to go off at random (all at once) during the school day. Each time, every principal was to write down on a card what he or she was doing; at the end of the day the actions were to be entered into a logbook and elaborated on as necessary.

As you might imagine, after a few days of this the principals were close to revolting; but what makes this study so interesting are the specific action vignettes recorded by the researchers. One of the best involved two principals, whose actions were compared when the beepers went off at about 3:15 pm. What are most principals doing at that time? It is a good bet that they are dealing with school busses, and one wrote, "3:15—Supervising school bus loading" on his card. Another wrote "3:15—Working with kids to encourage and raise expectations of success as they board the busses.

The contrast between these principals' actions and the way they interpreted those actions is striking. One was attending to bureaucratic linkages, dealing—effectively, one assumes—with the usual administrative problems of scheduling and loading school busses. The other was doing this while at the same time and through some of the same behaviors building cultural linkages, expressing values. The first principal is the sort who might carefully schedule a minimum of 51 percent of his time for "instructional leadership activities." The second is already spending 100 percent of her time as a school leader. We can now see more clearly just why the Illinois law cited at the beginning of this chapter is off base—principals should be instructional leaders not 51 percent of the time but 100 percent of the time, *all* the time.

All too many principals spend most or all their time building bureaucratic linkages. This is "level one" leadership, or management. It varies from bureaucratic ritual at worst to effective management at best. It is never the sort of leadership needed for effective—let alone excellent—schools. Level one leadership meets the needs of schools that do not exist today—if they ever did. Some call it the "egg-crate" theory of school organization, that is, the notion that each class is a wholly independent and autonomous entity and the only reason that classes meet in one building is for economy of scale in heating, hiring, and so on. Level one leadership is necessary, but it is not enough. The five strategic issues must be attended to not just in a superficial manner but at a deeper level of action as well.

To the extent that a principal engages at least some truly difficult problems in strategic culture building—the more subtle second level of the two levels of issues and tactics identified with respect to the five strategies—that principal is engaged in "level two" leadership, instructional leadership. This means doing the right things (or at least, many of them) while doing them right. This is a matter of degree; a principal might use one or two of the strategies, doing most things right and some right things, as well. Unlike level one management, level two is a form of leadership. It is, however, leadership better suited to a "factory/production line" theory of school organization. In earlier and simpler times this sort of simple linear planning model made sense for schools, as for factories. It is grossly inadequate for both schools and factories in today's complex organizational society.

Consider, finally, the principal who does things right, and does the right things right, and does so while using these actions to express and embed in the school's culture the values and vision that define and guide such actions. This would almost certainly mean using all five of the culture-building strategies, not just in their superficial first-level aspects but in their more subtle and difficult second-level manner as well. It is just this sort of leadership that is needed to manage change, deal with the unpredictable, and operate with real teamwork and collaboration. Such leadership is evidenced by the behaviors assessed by the LBQ, as reported in the first part of this paper. It is "level three" leadership, school leadership. Recall Ray Murdock, who expressed caring for the children while doing cafeteria duty and who, in myriad other ways, exhibited level three school leadership. Remember Frances Hedges, who created an opportunity for teachers to participate in a ritual that reinforced the importance of student reading achievement while she patrolled the halls and who, like Murdock, engaged in many, many other level three leadership activities. Level three leadership is appropriate for a *culture-driven* theory of school organization.

One way to think about these three levels of leadership is to imagine that level one leadership represents the overt textual material of leadership, the concrete fabric of which culture is made. Level two is the "subtext," the messages woven into the fabric. Not always easy to discern, these are nonetheless the "stuff" of which meaning is made. And level three represents the integrative, interpretive analysis that tells us about the larger picture, pulling together the various messages and meanings, helping people to perceive not a crazy quilt but a complete and coherent tapestry.

QUALITATIVE ANALYSIS OF SCHOOL LEADERSHIP: SOME CONCLUSIONS

The five strategies, used consistently and fully (that is, in both obvious and subtle manifestations), are major tools of school leaders. And when leaders skillfully apply these strategies, effective school cultures are built. There is no easy or simple way to do this; in fact, there is still more to the nature and task of leadership than has been described here. We are beginning, through careful observational research, to understand both the nature of successful school leadership and, just as important, how it can be applied. Qualitative analyses, like Deal and Peterson's (1990), on which we have built our argument, are crucial. Through such analyses we can understand, in a practical way, just how school leaders go about using the behaviors that are assessed in quantitative terms by the LBQ and that result in effective cultures as measured by the School Culture Assessment Questionnaire. The next step, of course, is to develop better methods for teaching both aspiring and current principals how to think about and how to construct school cultures of excellence.

QUALITATIVE AND QUANTITATIVE RESEARCH ON SCHOOL LEADERSHIP: SOME CONCLUSIONS

In this chapter we have tried to show in both concept and action that the qualitative and the quantitative aspects of research on school leadership are complementary rather than alternative (and sometimes contradictory) ways of looking at school leadership. We suggest that we must identify the behavior categories of effective visionary leadership and must measure both personal characteristics and culture itself. The evidence presented here gives solid support to the general concepts of transformational leadership as applied in schools and to the specific concepts of visionary leadership developed by Sashkin (1988a, b; 1989) and his associates (Sashkin and Fulmer, 1987; Sashkin and Burke, 1990). Visionary leadership theory is a sound base for understanding the "why" of effective school leadership.

We also believe that the knowledge gained can be effectively applied only if we understand the perhaps unquantifiable "how" of leadership. This calls for the sort of qualitative analysis illustrated by Deal and Peterson (1990) and presented in the second part of this report.

Ultimately these two aspects of leadership, the qualitative and the quantitative, *must* be integrated if we are to have a conceptually coherent and practically productive approach to school improvement through leadership and culture change. The work described here is an initial effort toward that aim.

REFERENCES

Argyris, Chris, and Schön, Donald A. *Theory in Practice: Increasing Professional Effectiveness*. San Francisco: Jossey-Bass, 1974.

Bandura, Albert. *Social Learning Theory*. Englewood Cliffs, N.J.: Prentice-Hall, 1977.

Bass, Bernard M. *Leadership and Performance beyond Expectations*. New York: Free Press, 1985.

Bennis, Warren G. "The Four Competencies of Leadership," *Training and Development Journal* 38, no. 8 (1984): 15–18.

Bennis, Warren G., and Nanus, Burt. *Leaders: The Strategies for Taking Charge*. New York: Harper & Row, 1985.

Bolman, Lee G., and Deal, Terrence E. *Modern Approaches to Understanding and Managing Organizations*. San Francisco: Jossey-Bass, 1984.

Bossert, Steven T. "Effective Elementary Schools." In *Reaching for Excellence*, edited by R. M. J. Kyle. Washington, D.C.: U. S. Government Printing Office, 1985.

Burns, J. M. *Leadership*. New York: Harper & Row, 1978.

Deal, Terrence E. "The Culture of Schools." In *Leadership: Examining the Choice*, edited by Linda T. Sheive and Marian B. Schoenheit. Alexandria, Va.: Association for Supervision and Curriculum Development, 1987. (Also, reprinted as Chapter 1 in this volume.)

Deal, Terrence, and Kennedy, Allan. *Corporate Cultures: The Rites and Rituals of Corporate Life*. Reading, Mass.: Addison-Wesley, 1982.

Deal, Terrence E., and Peterson, Kent D. *The Principal's Role in Shaping School Culture*. Washington, D.C.: U. S. Governing Printing Office, 1990.

Dwyer, David C.; Lee, Ginny V.; Barnett, Bruce G.; Filby, Nikola N.; and Rowan,

Bryan. *Frances Hedges and Orchard Park Elementary School: Instructional Leadership in a Stable Urban Setting.* San Francisco: Far West Laboratory for Educational Research and Development, 1984a.

Dwyer, David C.; Lee, Ginny V.; Barnett, Bruce G.; Filby, Nikola N.; and Rowan, Bryan. *Ray Murdock and Jefferson Elementary School: Instructional Leadership in a Rural Setting.* San Francisco: Far West Laboratory for Educational Research and Development, 1984b.

Edmonds, Ronald. "Some Schools Work and More Can," *Social Policy* 9 (1979): 28–32.

Firestone, William A., and Wilson, Bruce. "Using Bureaucratic and Cultural Linkages to Improve Instruction: The Principal's Contribution," *Educational Administration Quarterly* 21 (1985): 17–30.

Jaques, Elliot. "The Development of Intellectual Capability," *Journal of Applied Behavioral Science* 22 (1986): 361–383.

McClelland, David C., and Burnham, David H. "Power Is the Great Motivator," *Harvard Business Review* 54, no. 2 (1976): 100–110.

McPhee, John. *The Headmaster.* New York: Farrar, Straus, and Giroux, 1966.

Maier, Norman R. F. *Problem-solving Discussions and Conferences.* New York: McGraw-Hill, 1963.

Parsons, Talcott. *Structure and Process in Modern Societies.* New York: Free Press, 1960.

Perrow, Charles. *Organizational Analysis.* Belmont, Calif.: Brooks/Cole, 1970.

Peters, Thomas J., and Waterman, Robert H., Jr. *In Search of Excellence: Lessons from America's Best Run Companies.* New York: Harper and Row, 1982.

Purkey, Stuart C., and Smith, Marshall S. "Effective Schools: A Review," *Elementary School Journal* 83 (1983): 427–452.

Sashkin, Marshall. "Explaining Excellence in Leadership in Light of Parsonian Theory." Paper presented at the Annual Meeting of the American Educational Research Association, Washington, D.C., 1987.

Sashkin, Marshall. "The Visionary Principal: School Leadership for the Next Century," *Education and Urban Society* 20 (1988a): 239–249.

Sashkin, Marshall. *The Leader Behavior Questionnaire: The Visionary Leader,* 3rd ed. King of Prussia, Penn.: Organization Design and Development, 1988b.

Sashkin, Marshall. *Managing Conflict Constructively.* King of Prussia, Penn.: Organization Design and Development, 1989.

Sashkin, Marshall, and Burke, W. Warner. "Understanding and Assessing Organizational Leadership." In *Measures of Leadership,* edited by Kenneth E. Clark and Miriam B. Clark, pp. 297–325. West Orange, N.J.: Leadership Library of America, 1990.

Sashkin, Marshall, and Fulmer, Robert M. "Toward an Organizational Leadership Theory." In *Emerging Leadership Vistas,* edited by James G. Hunt, B. R. Baliga, H. Peter Dachler, and Chester A. Schriesheim. Lexington, Mass.: Lexington Books, 1987.

Sashkin, Marshall, and Morris, William C. *Experiencing Management.* Reading, Mass.: Addison-Wesley, 1987.

Sashkin, Marshall, and Williams, Richard L. "Does Fairness Make a Difference?" *Organizational Dynamics* 19, no. 2 (1990): 56–71.

Schein, Edgar H. *Organizational Culture and Leadership*. San Francisco: Jossey-Bass, 1985.

Sergiovanni, Thomas. *The Principalship*. Newton, Mass.: Allyn & Bacon, 1987.

Sheive, Linda T., and Schoenheit, Marian B. *Leadership: Examining the Elusive*. Alexandria, Va.: Association for Supervision and Curriculum Development, 1987.

Stogdill, Ralph M. "The Trait Approach to the Study of Educational Leadership." In *Leadership: The Science and the Art Today*, edited by Luvern L. Cunningham and W. J. Gephart. Itasca, Ill.: Peacock, 1973.

Thomas, Kenneth. "Conflict and Conflict Management." In *Handbook of Industrial and Organizational Psychology*, edited by Marvin B. Dunnette. Chicago: Rand McNally, 1976.

U. S. Department of Education. *Principal Selection Guide*. Washington, D. C.: U. S. Government Printing Office, 1987.

Chapter 8

CREATING A MASTERY-ORIENTED SCHOOLWIDE CULTURE: A TEAM LEADERSHIP PERSPECTIVE

Russell Ames and Carole Ames

Since the early 1980s, national- and state-level policymakers have taken legislative action to improve schools and students' test scores, and as a consequence, U.S. schools are experiencing major educational reform. These legislative prescriptions have tended to stress accountability, instructional leadership by principals, and curricula reform. In the Illinois legislative reform of 1985, for example, principals were mandated to spend 51 percent of their time as instructional leaders; a statewide testing program was established in reading, mathematics, and other disciplines for grades three, six, eight, and ten;

Based on the paper presented at the Symposium on School Principals, December, 1990, Otto-Friedrich Universität, Bamberg, Germany.

The writing of this paper and the research reported herein were supported, in part, by a grant entitled "Assessment of the effectiveness of school-site management: A recent structural educational reform" from the U.S. Office of Education, Secretary's Fund for Innovation in Education Program, Grant No. R215A93170. The opinions expressed in the paper are those of the authors and do not reflect policy or opinion of the U.S. Office of Education. Special thanks is given to Dr. Samuel Krug of Metritech, Inc., Champaign, Illinois, for providing and scoring the assessment instruments used in the research. Finally, this project would not be possible without the strong support and cooperation of the Illinois State Board of Education.

and statewide objectives were prepared to guide curriculum integration. In essence, legislation led to a "top-down" approach to reform, that is, state offices of education attempted to direct and control the activities of local school systems.

Recently, however, educational reform has begun to take a "bottom-up" approach, focusing more on collaborative and cooperative decision making between teachers and school administrators (McDonnell, 1989). In a bottom-up approach, the assumption is that teachers know what students need, and therefore should not be encumbered by state and central office mandates. The premise of this reform effort is based on American and Japanese business models that suggest that the best decisions are made by those "closest to the action," that is, those who will be affected by the decision (Peters and Waterman, 1982). Restructuring schools toward site-based management (SBM) has become the focus of these recent developments in the reform effort (McDonnell, 1989).

The central component of SBM is a school governance structure that relies heavily on teacher-based decision making. Within this structure, decision-making processes may focus on a variety of issues including the school's budget, curriculum, and classroom-specific factors. For many U.S. schools, these collaborative decision processes represent a distinct departure from more hierarchical approaches to school governance where principals do most of the deciding, and these decisions emphasize what schools need to do to comply with district and state regulations. Thus in the SBM school, cooperative teams of administrators, teachers, and sometimes parents and students work together to solve problems and implement solutions, and in effect, take over the instructional leadership function of the school (Duttweiler, 1989; Casner-Lotto, 1988; Chapman and Boyd, 1986; Goodlad, 1984).

Active collaboration between teachers and principals, whether or not it includes parents and others, however, is a relatively new phenomenon in U.S. elementary and secondary schools. In the United States, teaching as a profession began in the one-room schoolhouse where one teacher worked with ten to thirty students ranging in age from six to fourteen. From a historical perspective, the isolated nature of the teaching profession has carried forward into contemporary schools. Teachers are now assigned their classroom with students typically at one age level, although they are more likely than not to

group them by ability level within the classroom. Although cooperation between principals and teachers has been a rare event, so has
cooperation among teachers. It has not been uncommon for us to
enter a school building in April of any given school year and find that
a teacher knows little or nothing about how another teacher at the
same grade level conducts her classroom. Further, it is a commonly
reported experience that conversations in teachers' lounges rarely
focus on instructional issues.

Although there are many conceptual arguments for site-based
management as well as suggested action plans and favorable anecdotal reports from practitioners (David, 1989), there remains little assessment information on how SBM relates to changes in school leadership
and school climate as well as in classroom processes. This void in
research-based information led us to undertake a three-year longitudinal study to examine the effects of SBM, specifically on the cooperation of principals and teachers, school culture, classroom teaching
practices, and student motivation and learning. The remainder of this
chapter focuses on describing our study of these team leadership
settings. First, we address the fundamental conceptual underpinnings
of why SBM and its associated collaborative/cooperative decision
processing should lead to more effective teaching and learning.
Second, we outline the conceptual framework that guides our work
and provide information on the ·kind of assessment information we
have gathered.

THEORETICAL FRAMEWORK FOR SBM

Organization and Communication Theory Framework

As the reform movement has evolved, American schools have
been accused of being overly bureaucratic in structure, and as a result
organizational and management issues have become the center of
attention. School districts in large urban areas as well as those in
small rural areas have become increasingly centralized in their organization and control systems. In fact, some observers have suggested
that no organization in the United States is more bureaucratized than
are our school systems. Central offices of education have attempted to
control curricula, supplies, and hiring of teachers, and have allowed
teachers or schools little flexibility or freedom to change procedures.

In response to such centralized control, teachers often passively implement the mandated curricula with little enthusiasm or motivation, drop out of the teaching profession, or actively subvert the system. A common expression we heard from teachers subverting the formerly highly centralized central office for Chicago's school was "creative insubordination."

Most theories of organization argue that such bureaucracies are appropriate when the organization has few exceptions to deal with, problems are relatively simple, routines are easily developed, and constituents of the organization are relatively uniform (Emery and Trist, 1965; Katz and Kahn, 1978, pp. 259–270). The bureaucratization of the U.S. schools began in the 1930s with adoption of a "factory model," assuming that standardization was both possible and desirable (Presseisen, 1985, p. 16). The system worked reasonably well for those for whom it was designed—college-bound students. Many opportunities in the general workforce were available for the high school dropout (Presseisen, 1985, pp. 85–90). Although the factory-model school did not deal with the exceptional cases, that is, those who did not respond well to the standardized routines, the society at large had no real complaints because schools were meeting the labor-force needs.

Today's school environment has changed dramatically. Society now wants virtually all of its students to complete a high school education and to be prepared for some type of postsecondary education. There are increasing numbers of students who are educationally disadvantaged from the time they enter school and who do not have a strong family support system. It is a strong argument that schools can no longer ignore the exceptions and allow marginal high school students to drop out; they must now make concerted efforts to deal with these students (see Presseisen, 1985, pp. 86–88, 101–105).

Most theories of organization suggest that in organizations with many exceptional cases involving complex problems, nonroutine processes, and a high diversity among individuals, a decentralized structure is more appropriate. There is no question that in the 1990s, U.S. schools face a changing and turbulent environment, and will have to cope with nonroutine problems on a daily basis. Modern organization theory stresses that if an organization is to be successful within this environment, it must have multiway communication networks and a high degree of flexibility in the conduct of its work (see Forace,

Monge, and Russell, 1977, chapter 4). Communication structures in the organization must be established to meet the challenges of the environment and the purposes of the organization. Schools are clearly in a changing environment, and their current stated purpose is to educate all students to a high level of academic attainment. Forace, Monge, and Russell (1977, chapter 3) describe three basic types of communication needed for organizations operating in this type of turbulent environment: messages that (1) coordinate as well as regulate; (2) maintain feelings of personal worth, interpersonal relationships, and "organizational values"; and (3) focus on new ideas and new ways of doing things. The core of these communication structures are functional teams that work to solve problems. Communication between teams is facilitated by liaisons, and teams are reformulated as problems and goals change.

Until the present reform movement, team leadership involving principals and teachers, groups of teachers, or teachers and parents has been virtually nonexistent, except informally, in U.S. school organizations. There has been an overemphasis on communications from the central office that provide directives and that regulate practice, that is, rules and regulations about what to teach and how to teach. With little emphasis on staff development, the infusion of new and innovative ideas into schools has been slow. Further, given the isolated nature of the teacher's work environment, a new idea brought into the school by one teacher has had little chance of being used in another teacher's classroom.

Thus, while SBM is conceptually grounded in what appears to be the right organizational theory, teaching and administrative staffs are ill-prepared to implement the types of communication structures required to adapt to the changing environment. School organizations need to be restructured so that teachers and principals can work in small problem-solving groups in which they discuss new ideas and in which each member can come to believe that he or she can be effective in dealing with the challenging problems of teaching "difficult" or, at least, diverse students. The project described later in this chapter was designed to address some of these preparation problems and to field test an approach to overcoming them. Before moving to a description of that project, however, we move to the second conceptual underpinning of our work, motivation theory.

Motivation Theory Framework

In studying team leadership in SBM settings, we are interested not only in the motivation of students, but also in the motivation of all school-related personnel, including teachers, principals, parents, and support staff. Ames and Ames (1984) articulated a theory of *qualitative motivation* that applied to both student and teacher motivation and has since been extended to parents (Ames and Archer, 1987) and leaders (R. Ames, 1985). In this conceptualization, motivation is described as a qualitative rather than a quantitative variable. As a qualitative variable, motivation involves more than quantitative notations of energy or activity—it involves goal-directedness and specific cognitive-motivational processes. Thus, positive motivation is more than the expression of overt, purposeful activity; it is reflected in how persons think about themselves, their goals, their tasks, and their performance. Further, it is assumed that motivation among principals, teachers, parents, and students is reciprocal and cyclical; as teachers become more motivated to try new things, students become more motivated, learn, and achieve more, thus enhancing the motivation of teachers to keep trying. In addition, as teachers and students show enhanced motivation, the motivation of others involved in the educational enterprise—principals, parents, and support staff—is enhanced (Ames and Ames, 1984; R. Ames, 1983; R. Ames, 1985).

Our work suggests that there is a normative or ideal motivational state for the school learning environment. We call this environment *mastery oriented*. Whether student, teacher, or parent, when an individual is mastery oriented, he or she is focused on the process of learning as it relates to developing new skills and improving his or her own level of competence or skill. Underlying this mastery orientation is a belief that effort will lead to progress and learning. In a mastery-oriented environment, the emphasis is placed on working hard, taking on challenges, learning new things, and making progress (see also Dweck, 1986; Elliott and Dweck, 1988; Nicholls, 1989). Value is placed on learning and it is understood that the pursuit of challenging goals involves making mistakes along the way. When mistakes or problems are encountered, problem-solving strategies are enacted and the goal-striving efforts are maintained. Such a mastery orientation can be contrasted with an extrinsic motivation orientation or a performance orientation. A performance orientation places an emphasis on doing better than others and avoiding the public exposure of mistakes or errors (Ames and Ames, 1984; Ames and Archer, 1988; C. Ames, 1990; Dweck, 1986). Thus, a performance orientation is evidenced by the student who is overly concerned with grades and doing better than others or who gives up because he or she inevitably fails when compared to others, by the teacher who is more concerned with control and order than with experimenting with a new idea in the classroom; and by the principal who is so concerned with appearing competent that he does not share power with teachers for fear they will think him weak or incompetent.

The learning environment of the classroom or school can elicit these different orientations in students, teachers, and principals (Ames and Ames, 1984; Ames and Archer, 1988; R. Ames, 1985). And yet, the learning environment of the classroom and school is under the control of these very individuals. That is, factors under the control of teachers and principals can elicit either a mastery or a performance orientation in students and, unintentionally, in teachers and principals themselves. These factors have been enumerated in prior articles (see Ames and Ames, 1991), and include an emphasis on competition and social comparison, public evaluation, having high ability rather than putting forth effort, and recognition systems that make rewards available only to a select few. We have argued that many common classroom and school practices perpetuate a performance or extrinsic, rather than a mastery, orientation (Ames and Ames, 1991). These practices include, for example, the use of wall charts and displays that compare student academic behaviors and performances, the posting of honor rolls, performance incentive systems, summative rather than formative teacher evaluation practices, the public comparison of school test scores in the local newspaper, various forms of ability grouping and tracking, and the overreliance on tests of ability to select students for "gifted and talented" programs.

Because practices such as these are so ingrained in the structure of our schools, many schools provide only a weak mastery orientation for teachers and students alike (see Kohn, 1986). Yet we know that the development of a commitment to learning and an enthusiasm for challenge and hard work is extraordinarily difficult in schools where a performance orientation is dominant. Mastery-related cues are conveyed across many aspects of the school and classroom, from how tasks are defined and how students are grouped for learning to how they are recognized and evaluated. Similarly, teachers respond to cues from the principal and the school district that may or may not emphasize trying new things and experimenting (and maybe failing) with innovative teaching strategies. In general, it has been our observation that teachers are often reluctant to have their colleagues observe them for fear that a colleague will form a negative impression. A high school teacher once informed us, "The part I like best about teaching is I can close the door to my classroom and teach the way I want to teach without any outside interference." The values for independence and avoidance of public scrutiny are evident in the teacher's statement. Similarly, we have frequently observed principals who are afraid to delegate power, admit to a mistake, or try something new for fear they might be negatively evaluated by the superintendent above them and the teachers below them.

Although the norm in many schools appears to be a performance orientation, there are also many students, teachers, and principals who take a mastery-oriented view of the learning environment. Thus, we believe that it is possible to bring about radical change in this normative state of affairs. We believe it is possible for teachers to create a classroom environment where students see themselves as mastery oriented; for principals and teachers to work together to create a schoolwide mastery-oriented environment, and for the principal to work with those at the district level to encourage policies that support mastery-oriented schools. Thus, our work has focused on creating school environments where principals and teachers work together to create a schoolwide climate where all participants view themselves as learners who try new things, learn from mistakes, and focus on progress.

With this framework in mind—a framework that focuses on organizational communication and motivation—we now turn to a description of our three-year longitudinal study of instructional team leadership among principals and teachers in site-based-managed settings.

THE INSTRUCTIONAL TEAM LEADERSHIP PROJECT

This research has been guided by an overall conceptual framework as outlined in Figure 8.1. The key components of the framework are (1) instructional team leadership; (2) a school culture/climate supportive of instructional team leadership; (3) innovative

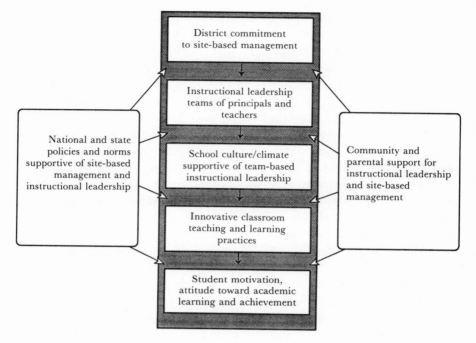

Figure 8.1

**Conceptual Framework for the Assessment
of Site-Based Management Schools**

classroom teaching and learning practices that result from instructional team leadership; (4) student motivation, attitudes toward
learning, and achievement; and (5) the school district and community
context of the school site. We began with the assumption that in SBM
schools, collaborative teams involving the principal, teachers, and
others (e.g., parents, students) can take on important instructional
leadership functions formerly carried out by the principal alone.
Further, we assumed that effective instructional team leadership results in a school culture/climate uniquely supportive of such collaboration. Finally, in schools with such collaboration, we would
expect to find a stress on achieving excellence, doing the job right,
trying new things, and improving productivity while at the same time
maintaining a strong cooperative power structure among teachers and
administrators. We therefore expect a strong emphasis on com-

munication that enhances quality of interpersonal relationships and innovation. Prior to discussing each of the five components of the model, we turn to a brief overview of our general cognitive-belief framework for understanding and studying leadership.

The Cognitive-Belief Framework for Team Leadership

Leadership has been described by many as involving two fundamental processes—getting followers to value particular goals and helping them identify the "means" for attaining the goals (Yukl, 1981). Getting followers to value a goal involves motivational processes, and giving them a means to obtain the goal may involve selecting personnel, providing resources, and training or instruction. Vroom and Yetton (1973) have suggested that when problems, like those in education, are unclear and complex, some form of extensive leader-follower consultation or group problem solving is necessary to maintain motivation and clarify the route to goal accomplishment. Most theories of leadership (Bass, 1981, chapter 19) suggest that when group members are involved in decision making, they become more committed and involved in decision making. In situations of high uncertainty, group problem solving can also help generate needed information—either new and creative ideas or simple sharing of ideas among the group—so that a higher-quality solution is reached (Vroom, 1976). Theoretically, then, team leadership approaches in schools should lead to greater teacher motivation and to better ideas for the educational programs of students.

We know from both casual and systematic observation that many leaders claim to involve others in decision making, and may, in fact, have many meetings with organizational members. Yet, these leaders can still be described as directive and as nonconsultative. Thus, even though there appears to be participation in decision making, the followers may not perceive that they are actually involved (see Bass, 1981, chapter 19). The question then is, How do we know when team leadership involving collaboration and cooperation among teachers and principals is taking place?

In order to answer this question, we have adopted the "social construction of reality" approach of Salancik and Pfeffer (1977) to understand and describe how individuals perceive their work environment and roles (see also R. Ames, 1985). The meaning that individuals ascribe to their roles and jobs is a process of social perception involving the mental process of gathering information about persons, events, and features of the work environment. When we ask someone about the quality of leadership in an organization or about their role in the decision making, for example, that person's answer is based on this social-perception process. The meaning of the leader's behavior to the followers and of the followers' behavior to the leader reflects the shared perceptions and beliefs of organizational members. Shared perceptions and beliefs are said to occur when many organizational members hold the same or similar views about the organization, including its mission and general approach to accomplishing its goals.

Thus in our framework, it is this "social construction of reality" that guides principal, teacher, and student actions in the organization. We look at organization members' thoughts, perceptions, and beliefs as the important phenomena in the study of leadership. By creating shared meaning of what is to be done, how it is to be done, and why it is important to do these things and by focusing on continual self-renewal and improvement, team leadership strategies ought to encourage others to act.

We operationally defined this sense of shared meaning as verbally expressed statements on a survey instrument. For example, the extent of shared meaning among teachers and principals in a school can be tapped by determining the extent to which they express similar attitudes toward such factors as the mission and goals of the school and the teaching strategies for accomplishing those goals. Thus, we would expect cooperative/collaborative approaches to school leadership to result in greater shared meaning as indicated by responses to our survey instruments. We now turn to a more in-depth presentation of each of the components of the five-factor model of instructional team leadership and the assessment of the shared meaning of these components among principals, teachers, students.

Instructional Team Leadership

Instructional team leadership is defined along five core dimensions that have been adapted from the work of Krug (1990). They are: (1) *Defines Mission*—the extent to which the principal consults and involves teachers, parents, students, and others in the discussion of school goals, purposes, and mission; (2) *Manages Curriculum*—the extent to which the principal involves teachers in decisions about curriculum matters including coordination of the curriculum within and across grade levels, ways to obtain resources to support curriculum development, and the improvement strategies for the curriculum; (3) *Supervises Teaching*—the degree to which the principal involves teachers in helping other teachers improve their teaching, including observing classes, demonstrating teaching strategies, and being supportive and helpful to each other; (4) *Monitors Student Progress*—the degree to which the principal involves teachers in discussions of student assessment data, including its assessment and the improvement of student learning; and (5) *Promotes Instructional Climate*—the degree to which the principal encourages staff to try out new ideas, obtain additional training, and foster regard for teachers among parents and students.

Our research has used the Instructional Leadership Inventory (ILI) (Krug, Ames, and Maehr, 1988) to assess principals' perceptions and the Instructional Climate Inventory-Teacher Form (ICI-T) (Krug, Ames, and Maehr, 1988) to assess teachers' perceptions of these five broad categories of instructional leadership. The ILI contains seven to ten items per scale that assess the principal's self-perception of behavior on these five core dimensions. The ICI-T contains a similar number of items per scale to assess teachers' perceptions of these dimensions. All items are rated on a five-point scale ranging from "strongly agree" to "strongly disagree." The internal consistency reliabilities, alpha coefficients, for each scale range from a low of .74 for "Manages Curriculum," to a high of .85 for "Promotes Instructional Climate" on the ILI, and all coefficients are above .84 on the ICI-T. The Instructional Leadership Inventory has shown strong concurrent validity in its demonstrated convergence with other measures of instructional leadership, such as the PIMRS (Principal Instructional Management Scale) (see Krug, 1990), and it has shown strong correlations with superintendents' ratings of instructional leadership and awards to principals (Krug, 1990).

School Culture and Climate

While the instructional team leadership dimension focuses on the specific behaviors of instructional leadership perceived by principals and teachers, the school culture and climate dimension focuses on the perception of more generally held beliefs and values by organization members. Maehr (1990) defines culture as the perceived "psychological environment" of the school. More generally, organizational culture has been referred to as the values, goals, and meaning of the organization that its members share. A strong organizational culture is said to occur when all of the individuals express a common purpose and believe they know what the organization stands for and what it means to be a member of the organization (Deal and Kennedy, 1982; Schein, 1985). Maehr and Braskamp (1986) took this very general notion of culture and defined it in terms of five goal stresses of the perceived psychological environment, qua culture, of the school. They define these five dimensions of school culture as including: (1) *Accomplishment*—the extent to which school members (principals, teachers, and students) perceive the school as stressing excellence and quality in what it does and as supportive of new ideas and innovation, (2) *Recognition*—whether school members believe they are given incentives and rewarded for working hard and for productive behavior and receive feedback about how well they are doing, (3) *Power*—the degree to which school members think the school environment necessitates competition for resources and rewards, (4) *Affiliation*—the extent to which school members are involved in decision making, have informal and frequent communication, and perceive a high degree of mutual trust and respect, (5) *Strength of Climate*—the degree to which members believe there is a shared view of the school. These dimensions of school culture are assessed on the School Administrator Assessment Survey (SAAS) for principals (Krug, Ames, and Maehr, 1988), on the ICI-T for teachers, and on a student version of the ICI-S. Each scale contains five to ten items, and the internal consistency reliabilities are above .85 for all scales except Power, for which the reliability is .69 (Krug, 1990).

Innovative Classroom Teaching and Learning Practices

If instructional leadership teams are operating effectively, then a school culture that emphasizes risk taking and shared decision making ought to lead to innovation and the use of innovative classroom teaching and learning practices. C. Ames (1990) has developed a comprehensive classroom-based intervention designed to help teachers establish a mastery orientation in the classroom learning environment. (See also, Ames and Maehr [1989].)

This intervention first involved identifying a wide range of strategies that teachers could use in the classroom to foster a mastery orientation (Ames and Maehr, 1989). These strategies (e.g., helping students establish short-term, realistic goals; designing tasks for novelty and individual challenge; developing organizational skills in students; evaluating students for progress and improvement) have been described in the extensive research literature on motivation and can be readily translated into actual classroom practices. These strategies were organized within a TARGET framework. The TARGET acronym refers to six manipulable structures (task, authority, recognition, grouping, evaluation, and time) of school and home learning environments and was initially defined and described by Epstein (1988, 1989). Epstein's TARGET schema provided a way of organizing and grouping the strategies within the six structures and making the intervention program meaningful and useable. In one study, the intervention was implemented by elementary school teachers over a six- to eight-month period, and its impact was evaluated in relation to several indices of student motivation (C. Ames, 1990).

The research model itself was collaborative, and each participating teacher was involved in translating the strategies into a wide array of rather specific instructional practices. As a result of this initial collaborative effort, teachers participating in the intervention were given a rather extensive set of materials that provided examples of instructional practices within each TARGET area. Teachers' implementation of the TARGET intervention was monitored by weekly record-keeping forms detailing the type of strategy and the TARGET area used. The effects of the intervention were assessed for several groups of students. Of particular interest here were those students who had been identified by the classroom teachers as "at-risk." The evaluation of the intervention involved comparing at-risk students in the intervention classrooms with those in control classrooms on several measures, including learning strategies, intrinsic motivation, and self-concept of ability, attitudes, and perceived competence. In comparisons from the fall to spring, the motivation and self-perceptions of students in the control classrooms showed a decline. In the TARGET intervention classrooms, however, such a decline was not found. And at the time of the spring assessment, the at-risk students in the intervention classrooms showed significantly higher scores than students in the control classrooms on measures of learning strategies, intrinsic motivation, attitudes, and self-concept of ability (C. Ames, 1990).

Based on these positive results, the intervention appeared to offer a promising approach to changing classroom motivational climate. This intervention, however, was being accomplished without the active involvement of the principal. In fact, the intervention was essentially being led by a group of university researchers working with individual teachers in several schools. During the course of the intervention period, it became apparent to the teachers as well as the researchers that some schools had programs and schoolwide policies or practices that were not consistent with the framework guiding teachers in the classroom-level intervention. It seemed that if such an intervention were to be effective on a widespread basis and maintained over time, it would have to be integrated within the broader school context and become part of the instructional leadership role of the principal, with the principal and teachers working together. Thus, we devised a plan to incorporate the TARGET strategy intervention program into our SBM project in order to test whether school-based instructional leadership teams could replace the university researchers as leaders of the TARGET approach. We now turn to a detailed description of our study of team leadership in SBM settings.

THE STUDY OF TEAM LEADERSHIP IN SBM SETTINGS

With the cooperation of the Illinois State Board of Education, we situated this study in twenty-five elementary schools that are part of the Illinois Network of Accelerated Schools (INAS). These schools represent a substantial investment of the Illinois State Board in an experiment that stresses collaboration among teachers and principals. Accelerated schools are the brainchild of Henry Levin of Stanford University. In becoming members of the network, the schools have adopted the principle of school-based governance by a vote of 75 percent of the teachers and staff. Decisions about curriculum, instructional strategies, and organization of the school day have been placed under the jurisdiction of the building staff. These schools are distributed throughout rural, suburban, and urban areas of Illinois. They range in size from 280 to 800 students. The schools contain large numbers of "at-risk" students with an average of 75 to 95 percent Chapter 1 eligible students.

In order to create the accelerated school, Levin calls for a complete restructuring of these schools based on three core principles: unity of purpose, empowerment, and building on strengths. Thus, principals, teachers, staff, students, and parents need to work collaboratively to develop a shared mission, empower teacher decision making, and be involved in fundamental decisions about the school budget and curriculum and instruction processes. It is only with this team leadership approach, in a site-based management setting, that the professional staff can respond creatively to the unique learning problems of the students. Under the organizational and motivational conditions, the staff can create an instructional program that will accelerate them to grade level (Levin, 1989).

Our study was a three-year longitudinal assessment of the impact of team leadership in these school settings that had adopted principles related to site-based management. A sample of twelve Illinois elementary schools that were not part of INAS and that were not involved in any form of SBM or team leadership between principals and teachers were recruited to serve as a control group for the project. The schools in the control sample were selected because they showed similar profiles in numbers of at-risk students. The first set of assessments was taken in the spring of 1990, with subsequent assessments given in the spring of 1991 and 1992. The ILI, SAAS, ICI-T, and ICI-S were administered to a sample of principals, teachers, and students from all 25 accelerated schools and control schools. Over time, we wanted to assess how the SBM schools differed from the control schools on perceptions of involvement in decision making and other related indices of cooperation among teachers and principals.

At this time, only preliminary findings are available based on the assessment in the spring of 1990. At the time of that first assessment, a number of important differences between the SBM and control schools seemed to be evident. These differences were especially notable in the school culture/climate area and showed that shared decision making, experimentation, and commitment to improvement were the norms in the SBM schools to a much greater degree than in the control schools. Teachers in the SBM schools showed a greater degree of satisfaction and commitment than did the control teachers. The SBM teachers also perceived a strong, salient culture, that is, they believed that everyone in the school shared a common purpose and knew what that purpose was. Teachers in the SBM schools saw their school as emphasizing "accomplishment" more and as stressing shared decision making, experimenting with new ideas, holding high expectations for students, and involving parents to a greater extent than did the control teachers. Thus, the SBM schools tended to show greater degrees of principal and teacher cooperation. And, this cooperation appeared to be facilitating teacher satisfaction and a renewed commitment to helping students learn at high levels.

Students in these SBM schools held perceptions of the school culture that were significantly different from the perceptions of students in the control schools. These students expressed a strong degree of loyalty and pride in their schools, and like teachers, perceived what their school stood for. The students in the SBM schools also perceived a greater stress on accomplishment and the importance of doing well, and they showed a stronger sense of affiliation than did control school students. Thus, the impact of cooperation among principals and teachers to change the school atmosphere was being perceived by students.

Training Program for Instructional Leadership Teams

It has been our contention (see also Levin, 1990) that principals and teachers need significant training and development to help them work as a team that can influence the motivation and learning of at-risk students in the classroom. Cooperative activities between principals and teachers must focus on more than administrative and school governance issues—if these activities are to influence student motivation and learning, they must also focus on instructional issues. In order to enhance the capacity of principals and teachers to work together in instructional leadership teams, we designed a two-part training program that focuses on team building and the TARGET framework. Thus, as part of our three-year longitudinal study, we are examining the impact of a specific training intervention to enhance the cooperative efforts of teachers and principals. In order to evaluate the impact of the training program on the SBM schools, we randomly selected thirteen of the twenty five schools to participate in a four-day training program in August 1990. The other twelve schools received the training in the summer of 1991. Instructional leadership teams composed of three teachers and the principal were invited from the thirteen selected schools. We now turn to a detailed description of the team building and TARGET training that the teams received.

Team-Building Training. We designed the team-building training around the core principle that team building is significantly enhanced if teachers and principals share their perceptions of the "strengths" of the school and the "areas in need of improvement" (Dyer, 1977; Nadler, 1977). In order to facilitate such a dialogue, each team was given a computer-generated report of the ICI teacher and student data. The report showed the average responses of the teachers in the school to all the items on the questionnaire. The summary of the teacher responses also included items grouped according to the instructional leadership and school culture/climate categories of the questionnaire. In addition to the average responses to each item and scale score for each dimension (e.g., "defines mission," "accomplishment"), a distribution of teacher responses across four quartiles and comparative norms for a sample of over 750 Illinois schools (Krug, 1990) were presented. The training consisted of providing the reports to the teams and leading them through an interpretation of the data. The teams were then guided through a ten-step school climate improvement planning process that asked them to diagnose school strengths and problems and then translate these into specific goals and action plans.

Team Leadership for TARGET Strategy Training. Each participant was provided with TARGET materials for classroom use. The teams were given a framework for understanding the purpose and goals of TARGET, they were informed about the motivation concepts and strategies that relate to each TARGET area, and specific instructional practices that illustrated the strategies were demonstrated for the group. A second component of this training involved a teacher-based program for involving parents in their child's learning. The premise of this program is that parental involvement and the link between school and home is a vital part of any school-change program and that teachers can impact student motivation and learning not only by what they do in the classroom but also by how they involve and communicate with parents. As part of this training, three types of communication practices, the content of these communications, and practical applications were presented. The intent was to increase the instructionally relevant dialogue between parents and the teacher and between parent and child.

Planning for Instructional Team Leadership in the "Back Home" School Setting. The last phase of the workshop focused on assisting teams in planning a set of leadership activities that they would carry out during the first month of school and each month of the school year. Specifically, teams were asked to prepare a plan to share the ICI data with the entire staff and to involve them in a dialogue about the meaning of the data and planning activities that paralleled what the teams had done at the workshop. Second, the teams were asked to prepare a plan for how they would present the TARGET framework to their entire school staff and enlist the involvement of all the teachers in the school to implement the TARGET program in their classrooms. Specifically, the teams were asked to have each teacher sign a contract in which he or she committed him- or herself to use TARGET in the classroom according to a minimal schedule, to complete a monthly report form, and to participate in a monthly meeting held by the instructional leadership team. In return, members of our staff reviewed the teacher report forms and provided individualized feedback on teachers' use of the strategies. Anecdotal reports from two schools revealed that for the first time in many years, teachers stayed after school to work on class preparations for TARGET and they regularly met to discuss TARGET as an instructional program. Another group of teachers chose to meet on Saturday mornings with no additional compensation to discuss and share their use of the TARGET strategies. The effects of the school- and classroom-level changes on teachers and students are part of the evaluation program.

CONCLUSION

As evidenced by the fact that the entire April 1990 issue of *Educational Leadership* was devoted to reports of site-based-management projects, shared decision making among teachers and principals is the dominant focus of current educational reform in the United States. Many of these projects are focusing on school governance issues—who votes in elections and what kinds of councils will represent the faculty in the decision making. Aronstein, Marlow, and Desilets (1990) provide an example of one school that is governed, in part, by a faculty council with six voting members who are elected by their peers, with the principal serving as a nonvoting, ex-officio member. The faculty council is responsible for collecting agenda items, studying problems and issues, and presenting proposals. The faculty has the ultimate power to make decisions, and faculty meetings typically involve the presentation of a council proposal, which is discussed, modified, and eventually voted on. Interdisciplinary grade-level teams deal with individual student issues, curriculum planning, special education cases, and administrative coordination of field trips, report cards, and schedules.

While the above case is typical, there remains little assessment-based information on the effects of SBM, how SBM can be infused into the instructional mission of the school, or under what conditions SBM might be effective. This type of information is necessary if schools are to invest in such reorganization. Moreover, such assessment can provide the basis for informed decision making at the school level. We are using a conceptual framework that links instructional team leadership to the building of a school culture/climate supportive of collaboration among teachers, administrators, parents, and others, and we are examining the impact of instructional team leadership on students' motivation and learning. We believe that an inherent danger in SBM is too much focus on governance issues to the exclusion of collaborative leadership among teachers and principals to improve the classroom learning environment. Our project involves a three-year study that we hope will generate reliable, valid, and broadly generalizable assessment information about a model that includes instructional team leadership, school culture/climate, and the classroom learning environment. We hope the information will aid school districts in planning how to create a school norm for innovation and communication that characterizes principal-teacher, teacher-parent, and teacher-child relationships.

REFERENCES

Ames, Carole. "The Relationship of Achievement Goals to Student Motivation in Classroom Settings." Paper presented at the Annual Meeting of the American Educational Research Association, Boston, 1990.

Ames, Carole, and Ames, Russell. "Systems of Student and Teacher Motivation: Toward a Qualitative Definition," *Journal of Educational Psychology* 26 (1984): 535–556.

Ames, Carole, and Archer, Jennifer. "Mothers' Beliefs about the Role of Ability and Efforts in School Learning," *Journal of Educational Psychology* 18 (1987): 409–414.

Ames, Carole, and Archer, Jennifer. "Achievement Goals in the Classroom: Student

Learning Strategies and Achievement Motivation," *Journal of Educational Psychology* 80 (1988): 260–267.

Ames, Carole, and Maehr, Martin. "Home and School Cooperation in Social and Motivational Development." Research funded by the Office of Special Education and Rehabilitative Services, Contract No. DE-HO23T80023. Washington, D.C.: Office of Special Education and Rehabilitative Services, 1989.

Ames, Russell. "Teachers' Attributions for Their Own Teaching." In *Teacher and Student Perceptions*, edited by John Levine and Margaret Wang. Hillsdale, N.J.: Erlbaum, 1983.

Ames, Russell. "Adult Motivation in the Leadership Role: An Attribution-Value Analysis." In *Advances in Motivation and Achievement*, edited by Martin Maehr. Greenwich, Conn.: JAI Press, 1985.

Ames, Russell, and Ames, Carole. "Motivation and Effective Teaching." In *Educational Values and Cognitive Instruction: Implications for Reform*, edited by Beau Fly Jones and Lorna Idol. Hillsdale, N.J.: Erlbaum, 1991.

Aronstein, Laurence W.; Marlow, Marcia; and Desilets, Brendan. "Detours on the Road to Site-Based Management," *Educational Leadership* 47, no. 7 (1990): 64–66.

Bass, Bernard M. *Stogdill's Handbook of Leadership: A Survey of Theory and Research*. New York: Free Press, 1981.

Casner-Lotto, Jill. "Expanding the Teacher's Role: Hammond's School Improvement Process," *Phi Delta Kappan* 69 (1988): 349–353.

Chapman, Judith, and Boyd, William L. "Decentralization, Devolution, and the School Principal: Australian Lessons in Statewide Educational Reform," *Educational Administration Quarterly* 22 (1986): 28–58.

David, Jane L. "Synthesis of Research on School-Based Management," *Educational Leadership* 46 (May 1989): 45–53.

Deal, Terrence E., and Kennedy, Allan A. *Corporate Cultures: The Rites and Rituals of Corporate Life*. Reading, Mass.: Addison-Wesley, 1982.

Duttweiler, Patricia C. "Changing the Old Ways," *Journal of Research and Development in Education* 22 (1989): 2.

Dweck, Carol S. "Motivational Processes Affecting Learning," *American Psychologist* 41 (1986): 1040–1048.

Dyer, William G. *Team Building: Issues and Alternatives*. Reading, Mass.: Addison-Wesley, 1977.

Elliott, Elaine S., and Dweck, Carole S. "Goals: An Approach to Motivation and Achievement," *Journal of Personality and Social Psychology* 54 (1988): 5–12.

Emery, Frederick E., and Trist, E. L. "The Causal Texture of Organizational Environments," *Human Relations* 18 (1965): 21–32.

Epstein, Joyce L. "Effective Schools or Effective Students: Dealing with Diversity." In *Policies for America's Public Schools: Teachers, Equity, Indicators*, edited by Ron Haskins and Duncan MacRae. Norwood, N.J.: Ablex, 1988.

Epstein, Joyce L. "Families and Schools and Children's Motivation." In *Research in Motivation in Education: Goals and Cognitions*, edited by Carole Ames and Russell Ames. New York: Academic Press, 1989.

Forace, Richard V.; Monge, Peter R.; and Russell, H. M. *Communicating and Organizing*. Reading, Mass.: Addison-Wesley, 1977.

Goodlad, John I. *A Place Called School*. New York: McGraw-Hill, 1984.

Katz, Daniel, and Kahn, Robert L. *The Social Psychology of Organizations*, 2nd ed. New York: John Wiley and Sons, 1978.

Kohn, Alfie. *No Contest: The Case against Competition*. New York: Houghton Mifflin, 1986.

Krug, Samuel E. "Leadership and Learning: A Measurement-based Approach for Analyzing School Effectiveness and Developing Effective School Leaders." Project Report. Urbana, Ill.: National Center for School Leadership, 1990.

Krug, Samuel; Ames, Russell; and Maehr, Martin. *The Instructional Leadership and Climate Inventories*. Champaign, Ill.: Metritech, Inc., 1988.

Levin, Henry M. Presentation at the Illinois Network of Accelerated Schools Conference, Springfield, Ill., 1989.

Levin, Henry M. "Building School Capacity for Effective Teacher Empowerment: Applications to Elementary Schools with At-risk Students." Paper prepared for the Project on Teacher Empowerment, Center for Policy Research in Education, Stanford University, 1990.

Maehr, Martin L. "The Psychological Environment of the School: A Focus on School Leadership." Paper prepared for the National Center for School Leadership, University of Illinois at Urbana-Champaign, 1990.

Maehr, Martin L., and Braskamp, Larry A. *The Motivation Factor: A Theory of Personal Investment*. Lexington, Mass.: D. C. Heath and Co., 1986.

McDonnell, Lorraine M. "Restructuring American Schools: The Promise and the Pitfalls." Paper presented at a conference sponsored by the Institute on Education and the Economy, Teachers College, Columbia University, New York, 1989.

Nadler, David A. *Feedback and Organization Development: Using Data-based Methods*. Reading, Mass.: Addison-Wesley, 1977.

Nicholls, John G. *The Competitive Ethos and Democratic Education*. Cambridge, Mass.: Harvard University Press, 1989.

Peters, Thomas J., and Waterman, Robert H., Jr. *In Search of Excellence: Lessons from America's Best-run Companies*. New York: Harper & Row, 1982.

Presseisen, Barbara Z. *Unlearned Lessons: Current and Past Reforms for School Improvement*. Philadelphia: Falmer Press, 1985.

Salancik, Gerald R., and Pfeffer, Jeffrey. "An Examination of Need-Satisfaction Models of Job Attitudes," *Administrative Science Quarterly* 22 (1977): 427–456.

Schein, Edgar H. *Organizational Culture and Leadership*. San Francisco: Jossey-Bass, 1985.

Vroom, Victor H. "Can Leaders Learn to Lead?", *Organizational Dynamics* 4 (1976): 17–28.

Vroom, Victor H., and Yetton, Philip W. *Leadership and Decision Making*. Pittsburgh: University of Pittsburgh Press, 1973.

Yukl, Gary A. *Leadership in Organizations*. Englewood Cliffs, N.J.: Prentice-Hall, 1981.

Chapter 9

VISIONARY SUPERINTENDENTS AND THEIR DISTRICTS

Judith L. Endeman

Visionary leadership is a concept based on research of America's best-run companies. Numerous studies have verified the importance of strong and visionary leadership at the very top of corporate organizations. Studies by Peters and Waterman (1982), Bennis and Nanus (1985), Bass (1985), Sergiovanni (1984), Sashkin (1986) and others clarify the importance of vision, mission, and goal setting to organizational productivity and improved outcomes.

Most investigations of leadership and outcomes have focused on political, military, or business leaders. Only recently has research on educational leadership begun to see leadership as related to the organizational outcomes of schooling. In the early years of public education, lay school boards took care of most of the administration of U.S. schools. Principals were "principal teachers" with classroom responsibilities. As schools grew larger, more complex bureaucracies were created. The job of principal became full time; districts with several schools and a superintendent in charge became commonplace. The responsibility for organizing teachers and programs shifted from boards to principals and superintendents. "Leadership" of the schools by an individual became more common and a focus on school outcomes became important.

Educational reform platforms contain strong rhetoric about restructuring educational organizations to allow more leadership by principals and teachers in creating change and improving outcomes. Yet the structural and organizational changes that would allow this local leadership emanate in part from the superintendent. The significance of a superintendent's leadership in envisioning reforms and in leading and empowering others in the organization to create change has been overlooked.

Studies of effective schools have focused on the leadership of the principal in creating productive change in schools. Few studies, however, have focused on the school superintendent as important to the development of effective organizations, effective schools, and positive outcomes.

The research reported here investigated visionary leadership in school superintendents. It analyzed the effect that "low" visionary or "high" visionary leadership had on school district organizational culture and on student achievement. Demographics were analyzed to determine if they served as moderating variables in the study.

VISIONARY LEADERS ARE LEADERS IN A DIFFERENT WAY

A careful review of a wide range of research and scholarly writing on leadership revealed two different patterns of leadership. There is a clear contrast between traditional leaders as effective managers for maintaining the existing condition and leaders who focus on the future and who are effective in managing change and in developing organizations. Table 9.1 illustrates differences in behaviors and characteristics of these two types of leaders. (The items in this table have been derived from the research and writing of a number of authors, including the following: Bass, 1985; Bennis and Nanus, 1985; Burns, 1978; Deal and Kennedy, 1982; McMurry, 1974; Owens, 1987; Peters and Waterman, 1982; Sashkin, 1986; Schein, 1986; Tichy and Devanna, 1986, Sergiovanni, 1984; and Polak, 1973).

The contemporary view of the study of leadership recognizes the importance of vision. Adherents of this school of thought hold that the most effective leaders are those who are able to create long-term visions for the organization and who can communicate that vision. They build a culture to support the vision and motivate others in the organization to pursue the vision as though it were their own.

Table 9.1

Behaviors and Characteristics of Two Types of Leaders

Visionary Leaders	Status-quo Leaders
Articulate philosophy and decisions	Talk about daily problems
Talk about future goals and products	Talk about current business activities
Schedule a few crucial appointments	Have a tight, overloaded schedule
Make contact with employees at all levels: management by walking around (MBWA)	Meet formally with immediate subordinates
Work toward consensus	Work toward conformity
Pay attention to strengths	Focus on identifying and correcting weaknesses
Take risks	Play it safe
Are emotional and spiritual, urge employees to bring hearts to work	Are intellectual and rational with reserved, formal responses
Have an action orientation	Have a planning orientation
Spend time on trust-building activities	Spend time developing policies and procedures
Develop fiscal autonomy patterns	Have close fiscal control
Communicate with symbols	Communicate in writing
Tolerate uncertainty and ambiguity	Need certainty and clarity
Simplify ideas using easily understood language	Use complex, technical language to describe ideas
Use symbols and rituals to reinforce and create values	Use symbols and rituals to impress

Use a loose-tight philosophy; tightly controlling core values, allowing individual latitude on implementation	Use a tight or a loose control philosophy on issues
Use effective listening skills	Are effective speakers
Use an ad hoc structure for problem solving situations	Use formal committees for problem solving
Generate energy for change	Are concerned with stability and calmness

LEADERSHIP AND CULTURE

Traditional outcomes in business and industry are easily understood and often studied. They are bottom-line performance outcomes such as profit margin, increased sales, or improved quality of goods. In the theory of organizational development, human fulfillment is viewed as an outcome. Organizational culture is one of these human fulfillment outcomes that needs further study. In schools it is an outcome that could enhance or inhibit the bottom-line outcome of student performance and achievement.

A strong organizational culture in schools helps members of the group develop constructive and responsible attitudes toward change. It helps define roles and promotes group cohesion that leads to goal achievement. Organizational culture also creates shared technical language and norms regarding teaching and the use of instructional time. Most important, it creates a shared mission and commitment among all members of the organization to achieve the desired goals.

Research conducted in the last thirty years clarifies the components of organizational culture. Parsons (1960) indicates that for an organization to remain healthy it must attend to four critical functions: managing change, organizational achievement, coordinated teamwork, and cultural strength. Deal and Kennedy (1982) support the importance of school culture to goal achievement. Sashkin and Sashkin (1990) add a fifth function to organizational culture, that of customer orientation. Strong organizational cultures with these components create meaning and help teach people how to behave in the organization so that top priorities are supported.

Schein (1986), a highly regarded organizational development

practitioner, believes that perhaps the only really important thing leaders do is to create effective organizational cultures. School leaders who hope to achieve long-term positive outcomes need to be aware of and attend to organizational culture.

Deal and Kennedy (1982) provide a clear description of culture as an important element that should be addressed during organizational development efforts. Their profiles of leaders as culture builders include individuals who also possess the behaviors and characteristics that other writers call visionary.

The basic, or bottom-line, outcome of a school district is student achievement. The usual measurements are standardized tests that are seldom inclusive of all the learning goals of the organization. Nevertheless, test scores constitute one measure by which the public evaluates school success. Thus, how visionary leadership impacts the bottom-line performance outcome as reflected in standardized test scores should be studied.

The question can be asked, Do superintendents have an impact on school outcomes at all? The main outcome of schooling is student learning. Superintendents are at least two levels away from where learning occurs; both principals and teachers are closer. However, as chief executive officers of school organizations, superintendents are responsible for creating the vision and the mission, setting the expectations, and managing the culture of the organization. They serve the same function as the CEO of a company whose bottom-line outcome is profit or loss.

Fostering a shared understanding of the schools' mission and developing a strong culture and climate may influence the district's bottom-line outcome of student learning. A superintendent with high visionary characteristics may be more adept at creating a strong organizational culture that supports the mission of student achievement than would a superintendent with low visionary characteristics.

A STUDY OF VISIONARY LEADERSHIP AND SCHOOL OUTCOMES

The purpose of our research was to determine if visionary leadership in superintendents made a significant difference in the level of organizational culture in California school districts. A second purpose was to determine if there was a significant difference in student achievement between school districts with "high visionary" superintendents and school districts with "low visionary" superintendents. In addition, this study sought to determine if the differences in visionary leadership and organizational culture varied when demographic factors such as years of experience as superintendent, length of tenure in the present position, or academic training were considered.

Design of the Study

The original population for the study consisted of all California school superintendents from mid-sized districts (student populations from 1,000 to 50,000) who had been in their positions for a minimum of three years. All of the superintendents (105) who met this definition were invited to participate. They were sent a demographic questionnaire and two assessment instruments: one to assess visionary leadership and the other to assess school district culture. Useable completed assessment instruments were returned by sixty-nine participants.

The *Leader Behavior Questionnaire: Visionary Leader* (LBQ-VL), developed by Sashkin, was used to determine the level of visionary leadership in superintendents. The LBQ-VL has fifty questions and ten scales developed from the research base on leadership.

A second instrument, the "School District Culture Assessment," was based on Sashkin and Sashkin's "Organizational Culture Assessment Instrument." Modifications were made to let the instrument reflect the unique language of school districts, while still retaining the basic meaning of the questions. The instrument was piloted with superintendents and principals and revised before being used in the study. It was used to measure change management, cultural strength, organizational achievement, teamwork, and customer orientation.

A demographic questionnaire sent to superintendents was used to determine the number of years as a superintendent, length of tenure in the current position, academic background, and level of education. The effect of these variables on each scale of the other instruments was examined.

Individual superintendent's responses to the LBQ-VL were scored and the scores were placed on a continuum from lowest to highest on visionary leader behaviors and characteristics. Marshall Sashkin, creator of the instrument, assisted in determining the cutoff scores to be used to select two distinct populations from the low and high ranges of the distribution. From the sixty-nine superintendents who returned useable assessment instruments, twenty-three low visionary and twenty-one high visionary superintendents were identified as subjects. Their school districts became the districts from which further data were collected for the study.

Principals from these districts were sent the "School District Culture Assessment." In districts with ten or fewer principals, all principals received this questionnaire. If districts had eleven to twenty principals, a random sample of ten received the questionnaire. In larger districts, the questionnaire was sent to a random sample of 50 percent of the principals. Three hundred nine principals in these districts completed and returned this instrument, a return rate of 69.6 percent.

The California Assessment Program tests, given to all third-, sixth-, and eighth-grade students in the state, were used to assess student achievement. Scores were collected for the forty-four districts for the 1984–85 and 1987–88 school years. Any changes in the three-year period were measured.

Visionary Leadership: Findings and Conclusions

Superintendents, as a group, scored much higher on the Visionary Leader scale than did other management groups thus far assessed by the instrument. The mean score of the sixty-nine superintendents was higher than any of the means of twenty-two other groups of public and private industry managers, school principals, military officers, and chief executive officers (CEOs) of companies. Even those in the low visionary group of superintendents scored significantly higher than most other groups. Only the presidents and CEOs of small to mid-size organizations scored significantly higher than the low visionary group of superintendents.

The high visionary group of superintendents scored higher than any other group that had previously responded to the instrument. The mean for high visionary superintendents was 227 compared to a mean of 203.9 for the next highest group, the CEOs.

The results from the visionary leadership instrument show that superintendents perceive themselves to be more adept than other business and industry leaders perceived themselves to be in the ability to

1. Focus on key issues and help others see these issues clearly (Focused Leadership);
2. Communicate the essential meaning of an idea or feeling (Communication Leadership);
3. Demonstrate consistency and trustworthiness (Trust Leadership);
4. Express positive regard of self and others (Respectful Leadership);
5. Take risks, create challenges and opportunities for implementing their vision (Risk Leadership);
6. Demonstrate self-assurance and belief that they can have an impact on organizational outcomes (Bottom-line Leadership);
7. Use power and influence to empower others (Empowered Leadership);
8. Create and explain long-range, complex plans for the organization (Long-term Leadership);
9. Attain goals through coordinating the work of others and the development of shared values (Organizational Leadership);
10. Develop and inculcate values that will strengthen the organizational culture and support the vision (Cultural Leadership).

These skills have been identified by behavioral scientists as being important for organizational development and success. Superintendents who demonstrate a relatively high level of performance in these ten skills should be able to create the organizational change necessary to restructure and improve the effectiveness of schools. Awareness of these ten types of leadership may also help boards of education select superintendents who will be successful in creating positive climates and restructuring education for the future.

Differences in High and Low Visionaries. An analysis of the responses of the high and low visionary superintendents on the Visionary Leader Questionnaire revealed strong and highly significant differences between the two groups.

High visionary superintendents had significantly different self-assessments from low visionary superintendents. This was true on the total score as well as on each subcomponent. Table 9.2 reflects these differences.

Table 9.2

**Mean Scores of Low and High Visionary Superintendents on the
Leader Behavior Questionnaire (LBQ-VL)**

Leadership Components	Low Visionary Superintendents N = 23	High Visionary Superintendents N = 21
Focused leadership	20.13	21.81
Communication leadership	18.83	21.05
Trust leadership	19.96	22.10
Respectful leadership	21.17	24.14
Risk leadership	19.78	22.91
Bottom-line leadership	21.74	23.95
Empowered leadership	18.74	21.33
Long-term leadership	19.74	22.86
Organizational leadership	21.48	23.81
Cultural leadership	19.26	23.05
Total	200.83	227.01

The largest discrepancy between high and low visionary superintendents occurred on the components of

1. Respectful Leadership: the leaders' expressed respect for self and others;
2. Risk Leadership: the leaders' willingness to engage in what others might term risky behavior to ensure success at meeting goals and challenging followers to pursue the vision behind the goals;
3. Long-term Leadership: the leaders' cognitive ability to think in long time spans about desired conditions and actions needed to move the organization toward these conditions; and
4. Cultural Leadership: the leaders' ability to develop and inculcate in followers the values and beliefs that will strengthen the organization and support the vision for the organization.

These four components describe personal behaviors and characteristics that differ greatly between low and high visionary superintendents. High visionary superintendents demonstrate them at a significantly higher level. Whether or not these characteristics help or hinder superintendents as they lead their organizations toward a more productive future is yet to be seen.

Organizational Culture: Findings and Conclusions

After identification of low and high visionary superintendents, the next step in the research was to determine if visionary leadership had an effect on organizational culture and on student achievement.

The premise of the study was that high visionary leaders would create stronger organizational cultures in their districts than would low visionary superintendents. Statistical analysis revealed that high visionary superintendents rated their districts' organizational culture significantly higher than low visionary superintendents rated organizational culture in their districts. This was true on all five components of the School District Culture Assessment instrument: managing change, cultural strength, organizational achievement, teamwork, and customer orientation.

Principals who worked in districts led by high visionary superintendents also rated their districts higher in all categories than principals who worked under low visionary superintendents rated their districts. These differences in ratings were statistically significant in three of the five categories of the School District Culture Assessment instrument:

1. Cultural Strength: strong agreed-on values that help an organization manage change and direct and channel the actions of the people in the organization;
2. Organizational Achievement: coherent and shared goals, with attendant values that support improvement and quality in achievement rather than maintenance of the status quo; and
3. Organizational Teamwork: coordination of the efforts of individuals and groups within the organization, mutual adjustment to meet unpredictable demands, and collaboration to achieve common task goals.

These components promote efficacy, the belief that people have that they can control and change their environment. Principals working with high visionary leaders believed that together they could focus their energy and efforts on improving outcomes in the schools.

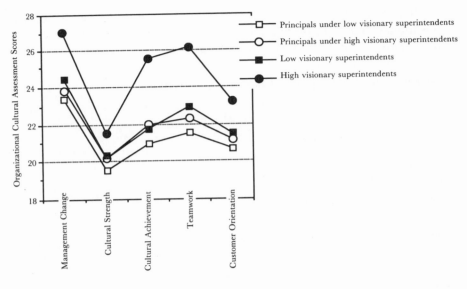

Figure 9.1

Pull Factor of Visionary Leadership

A common characteristic of effective schools and organizations is a positive climate. The three components listed above (strong culture, achievement, and teamwork) are the basis for creating positive climates and thus more effective schools and organizations.

Two explanations for these findings can be made. First, high visionary superintendents, through their characteristics and behaviors, create substantially different and stronger organizational cultures than low visionary superintendents create in their districts. Second, the propensity of high visionary superintendents to give strongly positive responses about themselves and the organizations they lead is contagious and is reflected in the more positive responses of their followers. The second explanation is similar to the "self-fulfilling prophecy," the "reflective phenomenon theory," or the "pull factor" of charismatic leaders (Polak, 1973).

When the scores of superintendents and principals are charted, the "pull factor" of high visionary superintendents is clearly demonstrated. Figure 9.1 illustrates this phenomenon.

The "pull factor" illustrated in Figure 9.1 may be explained by the higher leadership behaviors demonstrated by high visionary superintendents. As noted previously, analysis of the scores on components of the Visionary Leader instrument shows significant differences between low and high visionary superintendents in all areas, but especially strong differences in Respectful Leadership, Risk Leadership, Long-term Leadership, and Cultural Leadership. The higher ratings of high visionary superintendents may indicate the greater ability of these superintendents to influence their followers. They demonstrate caring and positive regard for themselves and others, they are risk takers, demonstrate self-assurance, and believe that they can transform the organization. Their followers become caught up in the positive vision and exert themselves beyond the level of followers in districts led by low visionary superintendents.

Principals working under high visionary superintendents perceive the cultures of their districts as stronger, more future driven, and more supportive of organizational achievement. They believe there is more coordinated teamwork and see themselves as important parties to the realization of the envisioned future.

Low visionary leaders with less forceful, inspired behaviors and characteristics seem to convey less trust. They may lead followers to be more protective of self and less apt to exert extra effort to achieve organizational goals.

Demographic Variables: Findings and Conclusions

No significant differences in the demographic variables considered in this study (because of their potential for influence on visionary leadership) were found between the high and low visionary superintendents. In other words, the two groups of superintendents were similar on all demographic factors studied.

However, when the variables of years as a superintendent, tenure as a superintendent, and advanced degrees were analyzed to compare within group variances of visionary leadership and culture, significant findings resulted. For example, high visionary superintendents with less than five years of experience scored significantly higher on culture building than those who had been superintendents from five to ten years. Those who had doctoral degrees scored significantly higher in visionary leader behavior, managing change, organizational achievement, and total organizational culture than those who had only a master's degree.

One explanation for this difference could be that the importance of organizational culture has been recently researched and reported. Those more recently in training for the position of superintendent would be more likely to be knowledgeable about the phenomenon. These differences may also be a result of the "honeymoon period" allowed new leaders. Before the political realities of the position have taught them caution, young superintendents may feel freer to express their values and to inculcate in followers the importance of organizational achievement and of the teamwork needed to achieve envisioned goals.

The finding that a doctoral degree was a significant moderating variable for high visionary leaders, but not significant for low visionary leaders, relates to the results of the Visionary Leadership assessment. High visionary leaders scored significantly higher than low visionary leaders on all subcomponents of the LBQ-VL, but the largest differences were in "trust," "risk," "long-term," and "cultural" leadership.

Those with high levels of trust and risk behavior may be more willing to delegate work and to follow intuitive or new ideas, including those learned in advanced educational settings. "Long-term" leadership is the ability to create long-term, complex plans for what the organization should become. This is an advanced cognitive ability that may be the key to successful internalization and use of the concepts learned in higher education. Those with high levels of this skill may gain more from a doctoral degree program than those with lower levels.

The results of the School Cultural Assessment Instrument of principals working with high visionary superintendents were significantly moderated by the demographic variables of "years as a superintendent (16+)" and "doctoral degree."

Principals working under high visionary superintendents with sixteen or more years of experience rated "managing change" and "total organizational culture" as significantly higher than those principals working under superintendents with less experience. A possible explanation for the importance of "years of experience" as a moderating variable in high visionary leaders, but not in low, is again found in the results of the Visionary Leadership scale.

Superintendents who have held their position for sixteen or more years have experienced significant changes in student populations and parental support. They have seen changes in funding structures, curriculum, and labor relations. High visionary superintendents have learned from these changes, have adjusted, and are able to convey this to their followers. Low visionary leaders do not convey the same knowledge and confidence to their followers. On the LBQ-VL instrument, the largest differences between high and low visionary superintendents were in the two components of "risk leadership" and "cultural leadership." The ability to feel and convey confidence while taking risks may make subordinates feel more comfortable while change occurs in the organization. Low visionary superintendents take fewer risks; they do not build as strong a culture to support changes as do high visionary leaders.

One explanation for the finding that superintendents with doctoral degrees in the high visionary group score higher than others in their group, while no similar significant variance occurs in the low visionary group, is that high visionary leaders are risk takers who accept ambiguity and are more open to new ideas. A doctoral education provides new ideas that are accepted and tried by high visionary leaders, while low visionaries may be reticent to act on these new learnings.

Student Achievement Outcomes: Findings and Conclusions

The basic premise of the research was that high visionary leaders would create goal-directed districts, which would result in improved student outcomes.

Mean standard scores in reading, writing, and mathematics on the California Assessment Program tests were collected from all districts. They were collected for 1984–85 and 1987–88 for grades three, six, and eight. Comparisons were made in four different ways:

1. Low visionary districts versus high visionary districts, 1985 (pre)
2. Low visionary districts versus high visionary districts, 1988 (post)
3. Low visionary, 1985, versus low visionary, 1988 (pre-post)
4. High visionary, 1985, versus high visionary, 1988 (pre-post)

Statistical tests were run to check the assumptions that the numbers and the distributions were standard. An analysis of the results led to the following conclusions:

1. Student test scores in districts with either low visionary or high visionary superintendents were not statistically different in the base year of 1985. However, the 1985 scores of districts led by high visionary superintendents were consistently, if not significantly, higher in each of the three grades and three subjects studied.
2. In comparing the 1988 test scores between districts with low and high visionary superintendents, one difference was found to be statistically significant. Student scores in reading were significantly higher in the eighth grade in districts led by high visionary superintendents. Again, scores in all subject areas in sixth and eighth grade were higher, though not significantly so, for the high visionary districts. In third grade, the scores for reading were slightly higher in the low visionary districts.
3. Over the three-year period, both the low visionary group and the high visionary group showed statistically significant gains in test scores in all subject areas in sixth and eighth grade. No similar significant gains were found in grade three.

SUMMARY

Some findings and conclusions can be drawn from the research:

1. The more significant improvements in student outcomes occurred in the middle-school grades in districts led by visionary superintendents. Organizational culture was also stronger in districts led by high visionary superintendents. Other research studies have found that school culture has a greater effect on school achievement as students progress from elementary through middle and high school. This study confirms those findings.
2. Perceptions of organizational achievement were higher among high visionary superintendents and the principals working under them than were the perceptions of organizational achievement among low visionary superintendents and the principals

working under them. This difference in perception may be a result of the increasingly higher scores, or the *value added*, as students move up the grades in districts with high visionary superintendents.

3. This research supported the hypothesis that visionary leadership creates stronger organizational culture and higher perceptions of organizational achievement and teamwork. Organizations with high levels of these elements of culture meet the human fulfillment needs of those who work in the "people-rich" business of education. These elements are also basic to positive school climate, a correlate identified in studies of effective schools. Seeking superintendents with visionary characteristics or training superintendents in visionary behaviors may lead to better schools.

4. Quantitative research support for the theoretical foundations of visionary leadership and organizational culture was provided by this research. A linkage between the two concepts was confirmed. Further studies are needed to clarify the connection.

5. The research found a high level of visionary leadership among the California school superintendents in this study when compared to the responses to the LBQ-VL from leaders in other fields. It also determined that high visionary leaders were more successful than low visionary leaders in developing strong organizational culture, in creating a feeling of organizational achievement in others, and in developing coordinated teamwork. These three behaviors provide a basis for district improvement and for efficacy, that is, the belief that people have that they can control and change their environment.

6. The study lent support to the theory that leaders with forceful beliefs and visions have a "pull effect" that causes their followers to perceive and create stronger organizational cultures than those led by low visionary leaders.

Superintendents who wish to strengthen the organizational culture of their districts need to recognize that there is not a quick and easy way to do so. It takes a focused vision that is articulated in a variety of ways. It takes shared development of values and beliefs that support the vision and its resultant goals. It takes the courage to risk making mistakes and the acceptance and respect of varied styles and strengths in the organization as long as they are goal directed. It takes involvement and teamwork among all stakeholders.

Superintendents wishing to take the first step toward restructuring and improving the effectiveness of their schools must look to organizational culture. They must create a work culture that is adept at adjusting to change, all the while holding firm to key values. They must keep always before them a clear vision of what the organization is to achieve. Through such vision will come the schools needed for tomorrow.

REFERENCES

Bass, Bernard M. *Leadership and Performance beyond Expectations*. New York: Free Press, 1985.

Bennis, Warren, and Nanus, Bert. *Leaders: The Strategies for Taking Charge*. New York: Harper & Row, 1985.

Burns, J. M. *Leadership*. New York: Harper & Row, 1978.

Deal, Terrence, and Kennedy, Allan. *Corporate Cultures: The Rites and Rituals of Corporate Life*. Reading, Mass.: Addison-Wesley, 1982.

McMurry, Robert N. *The Maverick Executive*. New York: AMACOM, 1974.

Owens, Robert G. "The Leadership of Educational Clans." In *Leadership: Examining the Elusive*, edited by Linda T. Sheive and Marian B. Schoeneit. Alexandria, Va.: Association for Supervision and Curriculum Development, 1987.

Parsons, Talcott. *Structure and Process in Modern Societies*. New York: Free Press, 1960.

Peters, Thomas, and Waterman, Robert H., Jr. *In Search of Excellence: Lessons from America's Best Run Companies*. New York: Harper & Row, 1982.

Polak, Fred. *The Image of the Future*. San Francisco: Jossey-Bass, 1973.

Sashkin, Marshall. *How to Become a Visionary Leader*. King of Prussia, Penn.: Organization Design and Development, 1986.

Sashkin, Marshall, and Sashkin, Molly. "Leadership and Culture Building in Schools: Quantitative and Qualitative Understandings." Paper presented at the Annual Meeting of the American Educational Research Association, Boston, 1990.

Schein, Edgar H. *Organizational Culture and Leadership*. San Francisco: Jossey-Bass, 1986.

Sergiovanni, Thomas J. "Leadership and Excellence in Schooling," *Educational Leadership* 41 (February 1984): 4–13.

Tichy, Noel M., and Devanna, Mary Anne. *The Transformational Leader*. New York: John Wiley & Sons, 1986.

Chapter 10

LEADERSHIP AND CULTURE: A QUANTITATIVE PERSPECTIVE ON SCHOOL LEADERSHIP AND INSTRUCTIONAL CLIMATE

Samuel E. Krug

Good scientific theory and effective practice ultimately rest on precise measurement. All science may begin in experience, as Cervantes suggested, but it does not end there. Science is concerned with identifying and explaining consistencies at levels beyond that of simple description or metaphor. Impressive advances in the physical and biological sciences during the past several decades resulted from an increased ability to measure the behavior of particles, planets, or cells and model that behavior mathematically. Similar advances in the social sciences will require us to quantify more precisely the behavior of those we study.

The past century has witnessed intriguing developments in the nature of the debate over the relative merits of qualitative and quantitative research paradigms in the social sciences. Initially, researchers accentuated philosophical differences that divided them, differences that had their epistemological roots in either realism (quantitative) or idealism (qualitative). For the quantitative researcher, an external reality exists that can be objectively studied and independently verified. The task of scientists is to establish general laws or explanations that increase our control over events. Quantitative researchers collect and analyze data in ways that minimize subjective distortion and personal involvement. The qualitative researcher, at least the early qualitative researcher, adopted a phenomenological perspective in which interpretations of social reality, not a single objective reality, exist. The task of scientists is to provide explanations and support them with rich descriptions based on extensive observations. To achieve such explanations, scientists must immerse themselves deeply in the context rather than abstract themselves.

As time went on, philosophical distinctions began to attract less attention than differences in techniques. In their introduction to research methods, for example, Strauss and Corbin (1990) define qualitative research simply as that which "produces findings not arrived at by means of statistical procedures or other means of quantification" (p. 17). They see no fundamental incompatibility when researchers combine quantitative and qualitative methods. They suggest rather that the researcher's training and conviction and the nature of the problem define the approach.

Thus, although the paradigms are rooted in two very different ways of thinking about reality, much current writing tends to ignore these epistemological differences. Many view them as alternative paths to the same end. Because the qualitative paradigm evolved later, some have begun to believe that the quantitative paradigm is outdated, inadequate, or inappropriate. The current move toward qualitative inquiry seems based less on the philosophical principles that originally distinguished the two traditions than on perceived inadequacies of the quantitative tradition. Some of these appear to have some validity. Other arguments against the quantitative tradition appear to rest on less certain foundations. Two of the latter, in particular, arise often enough to merit some discussion.

PERCEIVED INADEQUACIES OF THE QUANTITATIVE APPROACH

Quantitative methods are inadequate for dealing with real-life complex phenomena that are the true focus of social science. This argument appears in various forms and disguises. For example, quantitative methods are appropriate for studying the behavior of inanimate objects but not the behavior of conscious organisms. Or, much of what is important cannot be quantified; most of what can be quantified is unimportant. Strauss and Corbin voice a similar theme when they suggest that qualitative methods can be used to "uncover and understand what lies behind any phenomenon about which little is yet known" (p. 19).

Perhaps the most important conclusion to be drawn from the first century of scientific study on human behavior is that it is complex. (This is not a trivial finding. In other areas of inquiry, the process may have taken much longer. For example, it would be interesting to contrast contemporary scientists' confidence in the "laws of physics" with that of their counterparts of the eighteenth or nineteenth centuries.) A wide variety of influences such as learning history, the meaning the situation holds for the person, typical reaction patterns, current mood, and ability affect what an individual will do. Some have clear biological links; others have their origins in cognitive activity. Considering this complexity, it seems unreasonable to dismiss an approach for failing to attain 100 percent predictive accuracy in its first one hundred years. It is not true to conclude that quantitative methods are inadequate for dealing with complex behavioral phenomena. However, it is true that human behavior must be studied from a multidimensional perspective. The limited perspective of a narrow range of variables is insufficient to deal with that complexity.

Many illustrations refute the charge that important variables cannot be quantified. In the study of reading, for example, recent research tells us that a variety of influences, such as topic familiarity, understanding of domain-specific principles, and the reader's purpose, affect comprehension. This view placed a heavy burden on those interested in assessing these broad influences. During the past decade, however, several researchers have explored a variety of creative solutions to the problem. These efforts have led not only to fundamental changes in reading assessment but also to corresponding changes in reading instruction. Many other examples show that important influences can be quantified, although it may not always be easy to do so.

Quantitative methods require degrees of control over variables, people, and situations that cannot be realistically achieved. If we hope to understand the predictive relationships among variables, some degree of control is necessary. Otherwise, it would not be possible to discover causal sequences in recurrent patterns or choose among contending, equally plausible hypotheses. Sometimes effective control can be achieved experimentally. Many times it cannot. However, experimental manipulation is not the only way in which the researcher is able to achieve control. A rich array of multivariate statistical models allows scientists to achieve simultaneous control over the interactions of large numbers of variables that cannot be controlled experimentally.

Significant progress has occurred since the beginning of this century when Spearman first advanced his theory of mathematically defined factors that explained performance on complex cognitive tasks (Spearman, 1904). These sophisticated statistical techniques simultaneously consider the interactions of multiple variables. They eliminate the need for scientists to restrict their inquiry to a narrow range of variables in order to fit some imagined restrictions of experimental or statistical design.

Valid Criticisms of the Quantitative Inquiry Paradigm

Some arguments against the quantitative approach disappear under close scrutiny; others do not. Although these criticisms are not damning indictments of the approach itself, they highlight important problems in the ways in which some quantitative research proceeds.

There is a comprehensiveness and depth to qualitative studies that quantitative studies often appear to lack. The rich description and detailed illustrations that typify qualitative, especially ethnographic, studies are often missing in quantitative reports. Quantitative researchers are detached; qualitative researchers immerse themselves in their study. Perhaps this explains a tendency for some quantitative researchers to find the results of their statistical tests more convincing than do their readers.

Perhaps some of this is a consequence of the philosophical differences that initially distinguished the two positions. For the quantitative researcher, it may sometimes seem enough simply to present the facts because to do otherwise would introduce bias into science. Perhaps quantitative researchers' concern for discovering objective reality leads them to emphasize validity at the expense of credibility. However, results of a statistical test are not equally convincing to all audiences. Perhaps it is simply a failure of some quantitative researchers to conduct systematic inquiry. New surveys, questionnaires, and research instruments are too often constructed without adequate thought given to linking variables from one study to another. As a result, each study stands alone, and results and interpretations do not generalize readily from one experiment to another.

"Significant" results are often practically trivial. Statistically significant correlation coefficients and tests of mean difference are often much less compelling than some writers would have us believe. The use of

conventional significance levels in reporting results guarantees only that the findings are probably systematic, not necessarily important. Programmatic research that leads to a persuasive pattern of replicated relationships among a set of theoretically interesting variables is necessary to establish the importance of a set of findings. Unfortunately, programmatic research is not always the norm. Too often, quantitative researchers leave readers to puzzle out for themselves the implications and logical extensions of the numbers they report.

There is a balance to be struck. Perhaps this is what William James intended when he remarked, "The union of the mathematician with the poet, fervor with measure, passion with correctness, this surely is the ideal." The scientist should strive to provide both numbers and meaningful interpretations of those numbers. Perhaps quantitative researchers need to do more field work in order to make sense of the statistical relationships they discover.

Research designs often fail to meet fundamental requirements of quantitative methods. Statistical methods based on mathematical models of data can be stretched only so far. Assumptions regarding random sampling or assignment can be pushed to the limit when samples of convenience are used or when sample sizes are simply inadequate.

If we need to use a fifty-six-mile-wide accelerator to understand the behavior of subatomic particles, it is unlikely that a handful of measurements, however elegantly analyzed, will allow us to understand behavior. Most people probably agree that qualitative inquiry, with its emphasis on acquiring rich descriptive data, requires a substantial investment of time and resources. However, many forget that quantitative research in the human sciences is also data intensive. Because there are many influences to be considered and some can be only loosely controlled, the number of observations must be very large in relationship to the number of variables.

Quantitative research requires a substantial commitment to data collection, to data analysis, and to replication if conclusions are to be valid and useful. This is not always an easy task. Results are not always immediately exciting. This concept is not always marketable. But, this is science. The costs of such commitments have unfortunately led some people to adopt what we might call a *quantilative* research approach. Quantilative research begins with a limited sample size, often a sample of convenience, then proceeds to generate more correlations and significance tests than observations. This approach to research will undoubtedly produce conclusions: their validity is another matter.

WHAT RESULTS HAVE EMERGED FROM QUANTITATIVE STUDY OF SCHOOL LEADERSHIP AND CLIMATE?

Quantitative inquiry, properly conducted, can enhance our theoretical understanding of significant variables and our control over them. Consider, for example, the relationship between leadership and the climate or culture of an organization. Some writers use the terms *climate* and *culture* interchangeably. Culture as a concept includes the beliefs, behaviors, customs, and practices of a social organization. I use the term climate in this chapter to refer more narrowly to a set of beliefs or perceptions about the organization. Although it is reasonable to assume that there is a positive relationship between beliefs and actions, the instruments described later in this chapter assess only perceptions, not actual behavior. Many authors have suggested that the climate of an organization is an important variable that can be directed by leaders to achieve organizational objectives (Maehr and Fyans, 1989; Schein, 1984; Sergiovanni and Corbally, 1984; Walberg, 1979). Since 1985, an extensive program of research has systematically and quantitatively studied the nature of climate and leadership as it applies to the school setting.* Findings and conclusions have begun to emerge that have important implications for the preparation of school leaders and for school improvement. Here we will briefly discuss some of the key issues. (For a more detailed analysis of these topics, see Krug, 1989; Krug, in press; Krug, Ahadi, and Scott, 1991; and Maehr and Fyans, 1989.)

The study of instructional leadership can proceed independently of the study of school climate. However, our research suggests that in

* Both the Illinois State Board of Education through its Administrators' Academy and the U.S Office of Education through Grant R117C80003 to the Center for School Leadership at the University of Illinois, Urbana-Champaign, have contributed support for this research. However, the findings, opinions, and recommendations expressed are those of the author and not necessarily those of the State Board of Education, the University, or the Office of Education.

the minds of teachers, at least, there is very little difference between the two.

Our approach has been to investigate both instructional leadership and school climate with psychometrically refined questionnaires and survey instruments. A comprehensive family of instruments now permits us to assess and compare the perspectives of principals, teachers, and students (Krug, 1989). With respect to instructional leadership, there are five broad dimensions on which we focus. Each is briefly summarized in the following paragraphs.

Defines mission. People who score high in this area often discuss the school's purpose and mission with staff, students, and the school community. They take advantage of opportunities to stress and communicate school goals. Further, they try to make themselves visible in the school building and they communicate excitement about education to staff and students.

Manages curriculum and instruction. High scorers on this dimension provide information teachers need to plan their work effectively. They work to ensure a good fit between curriculum objectives and achievement testing and actively support curriculum development. Their primary emphasis as administrator is with instructional rather than administrative issues.

Supervises teaching. People who score high spend time encouraging staff to try their best. They coach and counsel teachers in a supportive manner. They attempt to critique teachers as though they were a mentor rather than an evaluator. They encourage teachers to evaluate their own performance and set goals for their own growth.

Monitors student progress. People who score high in this area regularly review performance data with teachers and use this information to gauge progress toward the school's goals. They provide teachers with timely access to student assessment information.

Promotes instructional climate. Administrators who score high in this area nurture learning in a variety of ways. They encourage teachers to innovate. They regularly recognize staff members' efforts, write letters of commendation for a job well done, and ask parents to praise teachers for their good work.

In one sense, these five dimensions can be thought of as key activities in which principals, as instructional leaders, engage. However, it is not easy to point to specific behaviors that constitute or distinguish each dimension. Consequently, it is easier to think of them as strategies that are discernible across a diverse array of behaviors or activities. Thus, writing in the staff newsletter, disciplining students, a Parent, Teacher, Student Association meeting, reading to kindergartners, and postobservation conferences with teachers all represent vehicles principals can use to communicate the school's mission and to nurture a climate that values learning. Similarly, there are many ways in which the principal contributes to the task of managing curriculum and instruction, supervises and supports teachers, and monitors the educational progress of students.

In the questionnaires we use, principals and teachers answer the same set of forty-eight items related to leadership practices. Principals tell how often they engage in that activity. Teachers describe how often such activities occur in their school. Typical items from the surveys include the following: recognize good teaching at formal school ceremonies (mission), review the fit between curriculum objectives and achievement testing (curriculum), model effective teaching techniques for staff (teaching), discuss assessment results with faculty to determine areas of strength and weakness (student progress), write a memo to staff praising their efforts (climate).

We assess the instructional climate of the school in a similar way. Separate instruments for use with principals, teachers, and students allow us to evaluate the same set of variables from each perspective. The variables are among those that research has found to be the most important in understanding organizations: accomplishment, recognition, power, and affiliation. Each is described briefly in the following paragraphs.

Accomplishment. High scores on accomplishment mean that the rater perceives the school as emphasizing excellence. They describe the school as being very supportive of teachers who try new ideas. Considerable latitude exists for creativity and innovation. The school emphasizes quality education and there is a clear focus on excellence.

Recognition. This variable assesses reinforcement systems within the school. When scores on this scale are high it means the rater perceives the school climate as valuing and rewarding good efforts. Productivity is very visibly rewarded and payoffs for doing a good job are readily available. Overall, the school's environment is viewed as a very positive one. The school not only encourages effort but also does something concrete about it in terms of a well-regarded reward system.

Power. This variable assesses the distribution and focus of energy within the school. A high score means the rater perceives the school as one that places considerable emphasis on competition. Conflict may occur often, but is probably viewed as a necessary by-product of competition. High scores do not necessarily describe a hostile and destructive atmosphere if the school consciously sets this tone in the hopes of encouraging maximum achievement.

Affiliation. When scores on this scale are high, a strong supportive feeling is felt by those within the school. Sharing of information, involvement in decision making, and mutual cooperative problem solving are some activities that describe the climate. Teachers and students feel that the school cares about them. Thus, words such as caring, sharing, trusting, and cooperating correctly describe the school's climate.

The instruments simultaneously assess several other variables relevant to perceptions of the school (e.g., strength of climate, satisfaction, and commitment). Again, the surveys contain multiple-choice items, but their content is very different. Whereas the first set of instruments assess the quality of leadership found in the school, these scales assess more general perceptions of the school itself. For example, to what extent are innovation and creativity nurtured and rewarded (accomplishment)? Is there an effective reward structure in place (recognition)? Is energy within the school directed productively or allowed to degenerate into conflict (power)? Do the relationships among students, teachers, and administrators rest on a foundation of trust and cooperation (affiliation)?

All of the surveys used have been carefully analyzed and standardized. Reliabilities of the scales are very high. A test is reliable when the scores it produces generalize or remain stable across some change in testing conditions. One of the most common changes in conditions to evaluate is that of changes in test items themselves. This is more usually called internal consistency reliability. The term refers to the expected correlation between one test score and a second based on an equal number of test items drawn from the same universe of content. Internal consistency reliabilities range between .74 and .85 (median = .80) for the principal version and between .51 and .91 (median = .85) for the teacher version.

A second set of conditions that is of particular interest from the perspective of studying social organizations is that of changes in respondents. That is, does a school score based on a sample of teachers or students from that school convey predictively useful information that can be used by planners to analyze and resolve problems? Would we get the same score if we asked the same questions of different people? For the study of organizations, a test score must generalize well beyond the initial sample of respondents if the score is to be very useful. Of course, not all scores will. To the extent that individual differences predominate over group perceptions in item responses, scales based on those items will not generalize.

That does not appear to be true for these instruments. When teacher surveys are averaged across fifteen staff members, for example, the results provide a reasonably stable, credible picture of the school (median reliability across scales for fifteen teachers = .80, range = .63 to .84). One would expect considerably more diversity in how students perceive the instructional climate of the school. However, comparable levels of precision can be obtained when results from twenty-five students are considered (median reliability = .80, range = .65 to .86). Of course, the reliability of the scores is directly affected by the number surveyed within a single school, and more precise estimates can be obtained as the number surveyed increases.

The development of norms for these instruments that reflect a diverse population of schools, principals, teachers, and students has been another major research goal. The use of these instruments in a variety of research projects has allowed us to accumulate results on several thousand administrators, approximately 10,000 teachers, and nearly 50,000 students (Krug, Ahadi, and Scott, 1991).

The development of a set of refined instruments has allowed us to untangle the network of relationships that link school leadership to student learning outcomes and to identify new ways of developing effective school leaders. The following section summarizes some of the things that we have learned and why they may be important for improving the quality of schools.

Perceptions of leadership and climate are very difficult to separate in the minds of teachers. Although the leadership scales we use focus on a much narrower range of behavior than the climate scales, teachers see an intimate connection between the two.

One approach we have used to examine differences between the two is factor analysis. This is a statistical technique that analyzes a large set of observations and reveals a more limited and fundamental set of factors that explain the relationships among observations. Just as a chemist analyzes seemingly diverse compounds into a set of common elements (e.g., hydrogen, oxygen), factor analysis could identify an extroversion factor, for example, within a set of items that involve sociability, warmth, daring, and congeniality.

When we analyze leadership and climate ratings made by teachers in this way, the line between the two areas appears to be very thin. In the same way that a common element, carbon, can be identified in such seemingly diverse substances as coal and diamonds, there is a large general factor that is common to teacher ratings of leadership and instructional climate. Teachers not only see an intimate connection among all five leadership dimensions but also find it difficult to separate them from the instructional climate of the school. There is an interesting parallel here between the way teachers evaluate student leadership and the way teachers evaluate student writing. Research has shown, for example, that various aspects of writing can be reliably distinguished, taught, and assessed. Maintaining topic focus, providing support for a position, presenting ideas in an organized fashion, and adhering to a grammatical structure that the reader understands are all important elements, but they are not writing. When teachers evaluate writing, they consider how students integrate the various elements, not just how they do in each category.

In a similar way, instructional staff seem less concerned with specifics than with the overall quality of the leadership, whether a coherent pattern is evident in the daily activities of school leaders, and the message the school's leadership intends to communicate. This would suggest that people who aspire to provide quality leadership need to spend less time on activity checklists and more time on why they engage in those activities.

Perceptions of the school by students, teachers, and administrators are independent, but interrelated. On the one hand, when we apply factor analysis simultaneously to the principal, teacher, and student ratings of instructional leadership and school climate, we find large rater factors. That is, three factors—whether the ratings come from principals, teachers, or students—explain most of the correlation among the original variables. On the one hand, this suggests that one set of perceptions is not directly dependent on another. On the other hand, there are systematic and important correlations across raters. For example, correlations between principal self-reports and teacher ratings of instructional leadership within the school are consistently positive. In addition, principal self-reports of instructional leadership correlate positively with teacher ratings of satisfaction and commitment. Elsewhere, I have reported that principal self-reports of instructional leadership alone represent about one-fourth of the explanation of why students stay committed to school (Krug, in press).

These are important relationships that have significant implications for understanding how and why students learn. When we consider the factor-analytic evidence in light of these findings, perhaps the best conclusion is that different perceptions are required to understand the dynamics of a school. If we focus entirely on the principal or on the teaching staff or even on the students, we may miss some key information that helps explain why students benefit from a particular learning environment.

When student perceptions of school climate are studied quantitatively, some interesting patterns can be discerned across the school years. While aggregating large numbers of student surveys across grades, schools, districts, and communities, we found a very clear but disturbing message in what students told us about their schools. Other studies have previously reported students' increasing dissatisfaction with school and have attributed it to student characteristics, changes in the school experience, or changing patterns of relationships with adults (Newman and Newman, 1978). Walberg, House, and Steele's (1973) survey of students in grades six to twelve suggested that dissatisfaction is greatest among ninth and tenth graders. They attributed the pattern to an increased emphasis on memorizing and decreased emphasis on innovative problem solving that peaked in the early high school years.

The data in Figure 10.1 represent the perceptions of students from districts located in four states: Arizona, Florida, Texas, and California. There is no guarantee that the sample speaks for the nation as a whole. However, the sheer size of the sample (N = 17,863) affords a certain degree of confidence in the conclusions.

In this study, we combined student ratings of school instructional climate into a single index of positive perceptions. Higher scores on this index mean that students see a stronger emphasis on quality, recognition, trust, cooperation, and shared purpose and vision. When we looked at the results, a general decline in the index across grades was immediately evident, although the raw data were somewhat uneven. When we considered the kinds of equations that could

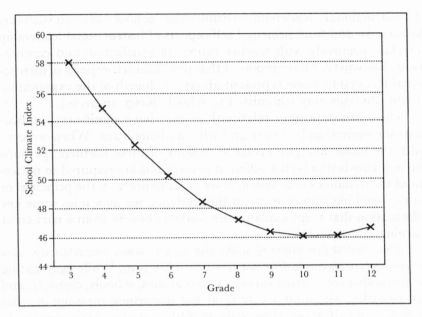

Figure 10.1

Student Perceptions of School Instructional Climate Across Grade Levels (3–12)

produce such results, a clearer picture began to emerge. We discovered that the relationship between student perceptions of school climate and grade in school could be represented by the following equation:

$$\text{Climate} = -4.64 \text{ (grade level)} + .22 \text{ (grade level)}^2 + 70.00$$

Technically, this equation represents a mathematical model of the relationship between grade level and student perceptions of school instructional climate, not a direct compilation of the data themselves. However, the correspondence between the scores predicted by the model and actual data is very high.

From the perspective of this model, it does not seem possible to conclude simply that students become increasingly disenchanted with school or that secondary schools are less effective at creating positive learning environments than elementary schools. This model allows us to see, more clearly than the original data, that two processes are at work here. The linear term of the equation represents one process. The quadratic (i.e., squared) term of the equation represents the other. The model further suggests that both processes are operating throughout the school years. This model requires us to search for theoretical explanations of what these two processes might be.

One possibility is that both a maturational (developmental) effect and a school effect operate simultaneously to produce the picture we see. As students mature, social relationships and other activities increasingly vie with school for their interest and attention. Although the school day may largely define the boundaries of a first-grader's day, those boundaries soon begin to shrink. Enabled partly by the instruction they have already received, students begin to participate more fully in a range of outside activities. School loses its attractiveness, not in an absolute sense but compared to other possibilities. This may be the story told by the linear term of the model.

The school effect, on the other hand, appears to counter this developmental trend. Perhaps the curricula of the third, fourth, and fifth grades do not meet the learning expectations of students who in their first two years learned to read, to write, and to compute, many for the first time. The diversity of the secondary school curriculum may reawaken and stimulate these expectations. Or perhaps the increased opportunities for social relationships through secondary school extracurricular activities help to reestablish in students' minds the value of school as an important place to be. Of course, some of the effect is undoubtedly explained by the fact that the most dissatisfied students have dropped out by the eleventh and twelfth grades.

We do not yet know what the final answers are. However, by going through this process of precise, quantitative inquiry, we see certain relationships and patterns more clearly than we could at the purely descriptive level.

SUMMARY

Epistemological differences aside, there is an intimate relationship between description and quantification in science. Inquiry usually begins at the simplest level of description. These attempts to identify basic features or characteristics of phenomena often lead to the development of taxonomies and classification schemes that help to organize our observations. This is a first step and a necessary step in the process of scientific inquiry. But it is not a sufficient step.

Consider, for example, depression, which has been said to have caused more human suffering than any single disease. Clinical descriptions of depression—or melancholia—by Hippocrates 2,400 years ago, by Plutarch 1,800 years ago, and by Pinel 200 years ago are strikingly contemporary and amazingly accurate. However, they are of very little value in helping to identify precipitating features in depression and to direct the course of therapy or to develop theoretical models that do.

Important findings emerge when quantitative inquiry proceeds systematically and programmatically. This chapter described such an approach to the study of leadership and instructional climate. The results have implications for developing school leaders, for creating more positive learning environments, and for creating more effective schools.

REFERENCES

Krug, Samuel E. "Leadership and Learning: A Measurement-based Approach for Analyzing School Effectiveness and Developing Effective School Leaders." In *Advances in Motivation and Achievement, Volume 6*, edited by Carole Ames and Martin L. Maehr, pp. 249–277. Greenwich, Conn.: JAI Press, 1989.

Krug, Samuel E. "Instructional Leadership: A Constructivist Perspective," *Educational Administration Quarterly*, in press.

Krug, Samuel E.; Ahadi, S. A.; and Scott, C. K. "Current Issues and Research Findings in the Study of School Leadership." In *Advances in Educational Administration, Volume 2*, edited by Paul Thurston and Philip Zodiates, pp. 241–260. Greenwich, Conn.: JAI Press, 1991.

Maehr, Martin L., and Fyans, Jr., L. J. "School Culture, Motivation, and Achievement." In *Advances in Motivation and Achievement, Volume 6*, edited by Carole Ames and Martin L. Maehr, pp. 215–247. Greenwich, Conn.: JAI Press, 1989.

Newman, Barbara M., and Newman, Philip R. *Infancy and Childhood: Development and Its Contexts*. New York: Wiley, 1978.

Schein, Edgar H. "Coming to a New Awareness of Organizational Culture," *Sloan Management Review* 25 (1984): 3–16.

Sergiovanni, Thomas J., and Corbally, John E., eds. *Leadership and Organizational Culture*. Urbana: University of Illinois Press, 1984.

Spearman, Charles E. "The Proof and Measurement of Association Between Two Things," *American Journal of Psychology* 15 (1904): 72–101.

Strauss, Anselm, and Corbin, Juliet. *Basics of Qualitative Research*. Newbury Park, Calif.: Sage, 1990.

Walberg, Herbert J. *Educational Environments and Effects: Evaluation, Policy, and Productivity*. Berkeley, Calif.: McCutchan, 1979.

Walberg, Herbert J.; House, Ernest R.; and Steele, Joe M. "Grade Level, Cognition, and Affect: A Cross-Section of Classroom Perceptions," *Journal of Educational Psychology* 65 (1973): 142–146.

CONCLUDING PERSPECTIVES

Marshall Sashkin and Herbert J. Walberg

The preceding chapters reveal the nature of educational leadership and school culture, and the ways they are related. Scholars and practicing educators have learned much about these topics in the last decade. We are now in a position to think about practical implications for educational leaders, especially at the school building level. In concluding we think it worthwhile to highlight a few key points.

For more than a hundred years educational administrators and policymakers have often focused on the more tangible aspects of schooling: building capacity, class size, and professional qualifications of teachers, for example. Finance experts have equated educational quality with the size of schools, their curriculum offerings, per student costs, and funding levels for special programs. All these objective indicators are relatively easy to measure. But what is measured now seems to have little if anything to do with the quality or effectiveness of the educational experience, for students or for staff.

Our intent in preparing this volume was to demonstrate that it is school culture, not counts of students, buildings, or dollars, that is a crucial influence both on staff satisfaction and on the learning environment for students. And school culture, in turn, is in large part determined by educational leaders, principals in particular. These assertions are not new; they closely parallel previous works in this series. In a volume prepared a decade ago on educational productivity and standards (Walberg, 1982), researchers could not easily show the linkage of objective indicators of school standards to learning. However, a book prepared about the same time (Walberg, 1979), reported research that clearly showed the influence of classroom morale or "climate" on how much students learn. Students' subjective opinions about the psychological and organizational qualities of their class-room life were related to their performance. And what teachers did in their classes had substantial influence on this climate. Several of the chapters in this book, especially the work reported by Maehr and Buck, reveal that principals, through their actions, can have analo-gous and substantial influence on school culture.

This book has addressed three broad but basic questions. First we asked, "What is culture?" Next we asked, "What is the nature of educational leadership?" Finally we offered several different answers to the question, "How do educational leaders construct cultures that lead to positive student outcomes?"

As for culture, we are still struggling with definitions and mea-sures. Are Deal, Maehr, Krug, Firestone, and Sashkin all speaking about the same thing when they use the term "school culture?" Certainly they are not referring to precisely the same construct, but is there enough similarity among their views to conclude that we are on the verge of having a clear and quantitative "handle" on the nature of this thing called school culture? We believe that there *is* an emerging general agreement, if not consensus, on the concept we label school culture. More clarity is still needed in the qualitative definition of culture, and more research is needed to focus on and assess the key aspects of culture. These authors are on the leading edge of these efforts.

At the same time that we are working to define culture we are only beginning to explore in the field of education what scholars of business management have come to call a new paradigm of leadership. Sashkin and Sergiovanni provide succinct synopses of the new "transforma-tional" leadership approach, an approach in direct contrast to the traditional reward and punishment, carrot and stick, model designed to govern transactions between leaders and followers. Sashkin argues that visionary principals transform school cultures by helping col-leagues adapt more effectively to their environments, focus on goals, and integrate their activities into a cohesive whole based on a set of shared values. Sergiovanni explores in more depth the underlying nature of these values and why they are so crucially important for improving school culture. But the suggestion that there is now general recognition of a clearly definable, if new, approach to leadership is premature at best. Scholars still argue about the nature of transforma-tional leadership. For some it is based on charisma and inspiration (Bass, 1985). For others it grows out of character (Bennis, 1989;

Sashkin and Burke, 1990). No common agreement is in sight, but perhaps none is really needed. It may be more important to understand the general nature of this new approach to leadership than to label or measure its elements.

Finally, we come to the integration and application of the concepts introduced in this volume. How do we educational leaders shape cultures? Firestone and Wilson look at two different but complementary processes, which they call bureaucratic linkages and building cultural linkages. Deal and Peterson are more focused. They concentrate on leaders' use of symbols, especially in the context of their use of ceremonies, traditions, rituals, and stories. Sashkin and Sashkin look quantitatively at measures of leadership and culture to demonstrate a relationship, but when it comes to how leaders actually construct culture, their argument becomes qualitative in nature, supplementing (and in some ways differing from) that of Deal and Peterson. Ames and Ames are even more narrowly focused on *team* leadership and its link to school culture. And Endeman shows us that this crucial leadership-culture link extends to the district level, exposing striking and important differences in the district-level cultures constructed by superintendents whose leadership approach is transformational ("visionary") or transactional. Endeman's research includes at least the hint of the effects that culture as defined and assessed at the district level has on students' learning.

So, how do educational leaders construct school cultures that have a positive effect on student learning? Do they build more cultural linkages by using symbols and ceremonies, as Firestone and Wilson suggest and Deal and Peterson detail? Do they hire people with the "right" values and use conflicts to define and strengthen new values, as Sashkin and Sashkin believe? Is it by means of teamwork that school leaders instill the value of achievement, as Ames and Ames argue? Or perhaps the sort of culture we speak of depends on the leadership of a visionary superintendent, as Endeman's work suggests. We believe it is all of the above. What culture-shaping leaders know, most of all, is that they must define, display, inculcate, and reinforce *values* because strong shared values define school cultures that lead to student success. All of the strategies and tactics defined and described by these authors are potentially useful to educational leaders who would construct the sort of cultures that help produce positive student outcomes.

Are some leadership actions more important than others for culture building? Undoubtedly. But we need more research of the sort offered by Deal and Peterson, by Sashkin and Sashkin, and by Ames and Ames in order to understand which. Are certain values more important in driving positive student outcomes? Certainly. But we must await more research of the sort pioneered by Deal, by Maehr and Buck, and by Krug before we can be more specific. Everyone wants a "how to" cookbook. The sad fact, however, is that we have no recipes to offer. Moreover, we seriously doubt that there can ever be such a guide to culture-building for aspiring leaders. At the same time, we believe that in this book there are more specific implications for how educational leaders can create cultures of excellence than are likely to be found in any other single spot. So, with all this in mind, we invite you, the reader, to take what you can use from our assembly of the latest research on leadership and culture and apply it to your own situation and your own needs. Despite the eternal need for more research, we are convinced that productive applications are possible and that they are necessary if we are to have schools that succeed in meeting the educational needs of the coming century.

REFERENCES

Bass, Bernard M. *Leadership and Performance Beyond Expectations*. New York: Free Press, 1985.

Bennis, Warren. *On Becoming a Leader*. Reading, Mass.: Addison-Wesley, 1989.

Sashkin, Marshall, and Burke, W. Warner. "Understanding and Assessing Organizational Leadership." In *Measures of Leadership*, edited by Kenneth E. Clark and Miriam B. Clark. West Orange, N.J.: Leadership Library of America, 1990.

Walberg, Herbert J., editor. *Educational Environments and Effects: Evaluation, Research, and Policy*. Berkeley, Calif.: McCutchan, 1979.

Walberg, Herbert J., editor. *Improving Educational Productivity and Standards*. Berkeley, Calif.: McCutchan, 1982.